Early Praise for *Vector Search with JavaScript*

Ben's book offers the approachable explanations and examples of vector search I wish I had when I was learning the field. It's a must-read for anyone joining my team.

➤ **Laurent Doguin**
Senior Director of Developer Relations and Strategy, Couchbase

The book does a great job at offering practical hands-on experience building applications powered by vector search. Ben guides you through a real-world project that builds on modern AI models for vector embeddings and integrates it into a functional application while also clearly communicating the underlying components such as cosine similarity algorithm and vector space.

➤ **Liran Tal**
Director of Developer Relations, Snyk

Ben is able to provide an approachable and thorough introduction to the complex world of vector search. His step-by-step guidance makes even the most overwhelming topics accessible, while his insightful comparisons of different approaches deepen understanding. This book is practical, engaging, and perfect for anyone looking to explore this transformative technology.

➤ **Kevin Lewis**
Developer Relations Professional

Vector Search with JavaScript is for everyone who wants to explore the world of vector search. The book implements a working vector search service and covers security and validation. This could easily be the best book on crafting an API using Node.js.

➤ **Santosh Yadav**
Staff Engineer, GitHub Star, Microsoft MVP and Angular GDE

Vector Search with JavaScript

Build Intelligent Search Systems with AI

Ben Greenberg

The Pragmatic Bookshelf

Dallas, Texas

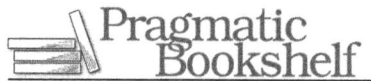

Pragmatic Bookshelf

See our complete catalog of hands-on, practical,
and Pragmatic content for software developers:
https://pragprog.com

Sales, volume licensing, and support:
support@pragprog.com

Derivative works, AI training and testing,
international translations, and other rights:
rights@pragprog.com

The team that produced this book includes:

Publisher: Dave Thomas
COO: Janet Furlow
Development Editor: Susannah Davidson
Copy Editor: L. Sakhi MacMillan
Layout: Gilson Graphics

ISBN-13: 979-8-88865-173-5
Book version: P1.0—September 2025

For my sons, whose endless questions and curiosity inspired this book and motivate me every day to keep exploring.

Ben Greenberg

Contents

Part I — Foundations of Vector Search

Part II — Building a Vector Search Service

Foreword

I still remember the first time I had to test a recommendation system powered by AI. This was one of the most advanced features our product offered. I was excited, but also completely out of my depth. As someone who was used to working with deterministic systems, I was thrown into a world where there were no concrete expectations—just probabilities and learned behavior. "Correct" became a range, not an absolute. And I had to figure out how to test it anyway.

To do that, I didn't just automate inputs and assert outputs. I had to train the system, simulate customer usage, and apply some good old-fashioned common sense. I had to challenge assumptions, ask better questions, and think critically about how this "intelligent" system was making decisions that affected real users. It pushed me out of my comfort zone, and honestly, I'm better for it.

That experience taught me something important. If you're going to work with AI, it's in your best interest to understand how it works, what it's optimizing for, and how those choices impact real people.

Vector Search with JavaScript is the book I wish I had when I first started working in this space. Vector search is one of those techniques that can seem like magic. But behind that magic are embeddings, similarity scores, and complex math. If you don't grasp what those pieces are doing, it's easy to misapply them or misinterpret the results.

Ben makes this topic accessible, practical, and even fun. He walks you through how vector search works, what embeddings are really doing, and how to build an intelligent search system that responds based on meaning, not just matching words.

This book is especially timely. As developers, we're being asked to integrate AI into more and more of our applications. Understanding what that *really* means is a competitive advantage. Ben highlights how real companies are using these techniques to make their products smarter and more helpful. He also reinforces your learning by having you build a fully featured app and apply vector search to realistic data, just like modern apps do today.

If you're a developer who wants to go beyond keyword search and start delivering smarter, more relevant results, this book is your guide.

Angie Jones, VP, Developer Relations

Acknowledgments

I'm grateful to the many technical reviewers who offered thoughtful feedback, sharp insights, and generous encouragement throughout the writing of this book. Their input made the work clearer, more accurate, and far more useful.

- Aisha Blake
- Brian King
- Josh Grossman
- Kevin Lewis
- Samhitha Prasad
- Tanay Pant

Thanks to Susannah Davidson and the entire Pragmatic Bookshelf production team for their guidance, patience, and attention to detail from the first draft to the final layout.

To my family, thank you for your support and encouragement in this project. And to my wife in particular, whose patience and support made the many nights and weekends spent working on this book possible.

Introduction

Welcome to the world of vector search! By opening this book, you've taken the first step toward mastering an area of technology that powers modern search experiences. Vector search leverages advanced machine learning techniques to deliver relevant, precise, and context-aware results across various domains. Whether it's driving the search bar on a website, personalizing content recommendations, or enabling cutting-edge anomaly detection, vector search redefines how we access and interact with information.

As user expectations for seamless and intuitive experiences grow, traditional keyword-based search systems often fall short of the mark. Users demand accurate results even when their queries are imprecise, support for contextual understanding, and the ability to surface hidden insights within vast datasets. Vector search meets these challenges by embedding data into dense mathematical representations, enabling powerful similarity calculations that uncover deeper relationships and meaning.

This book is your guide to understanding and implementing vector search systems. We'll explore the core concepts, tools, and techniques that underpin vector search and provide you with the knowledge and skills to build your search applications. By the end of this book, you'll harness the potential of vector search and create intelligent, efficient search systems that deliver value to your users.

Who This Book Is For

This book is written for developers who want to build smarter, more effective search experiences. If you're a back-end engineer looking to go beyond traditional search techniques or a full-stack developer curious about integrating AI into your applications, you'll find the concepts and code examples in this book approachable and actionable.

You'll need some basic familiarity with JavaScript and Node.js, but you don't need a background in machine learning or search theory. Every concept is introduced clearly, explained in plain language, and backed by working code. By the time you're done, you'll have both a solid understanding of vector search and the skills to apply it in your own projects.

What's in This Book

This book provides a hands-on approach to vector search, blending theoretical explanations with real-world coding examples. You'll learn how to implement vector search step by step, from generating embeddings to optimizing performance. We'll cover key concepts such as vector indexing, query handling, and hybrid search techniques along the way. Each chapter builds on the last, but if you're already familiar with specific topics, feel free to jump to the sections that interest you most; for example, if you're already knowledgeable on the foundations of vector search, you may want to skip Chapter 2, Understanding Vector Search, on page 11.

Throughout the book, you'll work on a project based on the RealWorld example app, a full-stack blogging platform that mimics the features of Medium. You'll enhance this familiar app with vector-powered functionality, step by step. By embedding content, enabling similarity search, and layering in hybrid techniques, you'll transform a conventional CRUD app into a modern, intelligent search experience. This project grounds each concept in practical, real-world implementation and serves as a running example you can adapt and expand in your own work.

This book is structured in two parts. Part 1, Foundations of Vector Search, includes Chapters 1 through 3 and focuses on the core ideas: what vector search is, how it works, and the building blocks such as embeddings and similarity. Part 2, Building a Vector Search Service, spans Chapters 4 through 11 and walks you through designing, implementing, and optimizing a fully functional search system using real code and real data.

Wondering where to begin? You'll get your feet wet with a quick hands-on vector search project in the first chapter. The second chapter will introduce you to the fundamentals of vector search, including how it differs from traditional search methods and a high-level overview of commonly used techniques. If you're already familiar with the basics, you can skip ahead to Chapter 3, Generating Vector Embeddings, on page 15, to dive into how vector embeddings work and why they're essential. Feeling ready to build? Head straight to Chapter 4, Building the Foundation for Vector Search, on page 25, to set up your environment and start coding your own vector search system from the ground up.

Conventions Used in This Book

This book presents all code snippets in JavaScript and formats them for easy readability. It highlights essential terms and concepts at first use and pairs practical examples with clear explanations. Diagrams and other visualizations support the text, while side notes and case studies offer additional insights to deepen your understanding. By working through the examples in each chapter, you'll gain a solid understanding of vector search and build a functional search system from scratch.

Online Resources

You'll find a dedicated page for this book on the Pragmatic Bookshelf website.[1] From there, you can download the complete source code.

Do you have feedback or questions? Follow the links on the book's web page to the DevTalk forum, where you can report a mistake, suggest changes, or just discuss what you've learned with other readers.

The author's GitHub repository is also at https://vectorsearchbook.com/. This repository contains the source code for the application built throughout the book and will be updated regularly for the latest tooling and library changes. You can also find additional resources and sign up for a newsletter to stay informed about the newest AI-powered search developments on the website.

Vector search is a technology that presents an inflection point in user experience. It's a gateway to building more intelligent, intuitive systems that can transform how users interact with data. By the end of this book, you'll have the skills to implement robust vector search solutions tailored to your projects. So, let's begin our journey into the world of vector search!

---

1. http://pragprog.com/titles/bgvector

Part I

Foundations of Vector Search

CHAPTER 1

Getting Started with Vector Search

Let's get our feet wet with a quick example project to see how useful vector search can be. You'll learn all about the underlying concepts in the following chapters, but for now, we're just going to have some fun and see vector search in action. Later in this book, you'll build a working vector search project from scratch based on a widely adapted open source project. This chapter invites you to work with real data, run real code, and see meaningful results before we introduce any formal definitions or math.

Imagine you're writing this book. Sure, writing the text took a while, but you managed to finish everything ... when all of a sudden you get writer's block. You need a title for the book, and you can't figure out what would not only be a great title but something that fits in with your publisher's style of book titles. That was me, and guess what, I used vector search to help me come up with just the right title for this book.

You now get to follow that same process. Using the OpenAI API, you'll generate embeddings from real Pragmatic titles, store them locally, and compare them to a title idea of your own. This exercise gives you a practical and approachable way to engage with vector search before we unpack the deeper concepts behind it. All you need is one file, a small dataset, and a willingness to explore.

Setting Up the Project

Create a new file named name_this_book.js. This file will do everything for you: scrape the website, generate embeddings, compare them, and return the top matches. Embeddings are numerical representations of text that capture its meaning and context. Embeddings are a central concept throughout this book, and we'll explore them in much greater depth as we go.

Before installing the required libraries, make sure you have Node.js installed. You can download it from the official website.[1] Installing Node.js will also install npm, which is the package manager we'll use throughout this book.

Once done installing Node.js, you'll need to install a few libraries:

```
npm install node-fetch dotenv cheerio
```

And you'll need an OpenAI API key in a local .env file:

```
echo "OPENAI_API_KEY=your-key-here" > .env
```

Scraping the Titles

We'll start by scraping all the titles from the Pragmatic Bookshelf catalog. Their site uses pagination, so we'll loop through all pages and extract the title, subtitle, and book URL.

Here's the function to do that:

getting_started_with_vector_search/name_this_book.js
```
async function scrapeTitles() {
  const baseURL = 'https://pragprog.com';
  const maxPages = 27;
  const maxTitles = 50;
  const allBooks = [];

  console.log(`
    Scraping up to ${maxTitles} book titles from Pragmatic Bookshelf...
  `);

  for (let page = 1; page <= maxPages; page++) {
    const pageURL = page === 1
      ? `${baseURL}/titles/`
      : `${baseURL}/titles/page/${page}/`;

    console.log(` - Fetching page ${page}`);

    const res = await fetch(pageURL);
    const html = await res.text();
    const $ = cheerio.load(html);

    $('.category-title-container').each((_, el) => {
      if (allBooks.length >= maxTitles) return false;
      const anchor = $(el).find('a').first();
      const title = $(el)
        .find('.category-title-title b')
        .text()
        .trim();
```

---

1. https://www.nodejs.org

```
    const subtitle = $(el)
      .find('.category-title-subtitle')
      .text()
      .trim();
    const url = anchor.attr('href');
    if (title && url) {
      allBooks.push({ title, subtitle, url });
    }
  });

  if (allBooks.length >= maxTitles) break;
}
const unique = Array.from(
  new Map(allBooks.map(b => [b.url, b])).values()
);
console.log(`
  \nFinished scraping. ${unique.length} titles captured.
`);

return unique;
}
```

This function loops through every results page, uses Cheerio, a JavaScript library, to parse the titles and subtitles, and returns a list of unique book entries.

You're now working with real-world HTML. Scraping is often messy and requires patience. The structure of Pragmatic's catalog is structurally clean, but keep in mind that websites can change. This kind of work is always fragile by nature. If the site layout or class names change, your scraper could break. That means your downstream processes, like generating embeddings or running similarity comparisons, might be working with incomplete or outdated data.

Embedding the Titles

Next, we'll use OpenAI's text-embedding-3-small model to generate an embedding for each full book title.

Let's define a helper function to generate a single embedding:

```
getting_started_with_vector_search/name_this_book.js
async function getEmbedding(text) {
  console.log(`Generating embedding for: "${text}"`);
  try {
    const res = await fetch('https://api.openai.com/v1/embeddings', {
      method: 'POST',
      headers: {
        'Authorization': `Bearer ${process.env.OPENAI_API_KEY}`,
        'Content-Type': 'application/json',
      },
```

```
      body: JSON.stringify({
        input: text,
        model: 'text-embedding-3-small',
      }),
    });

    if (!res.ok) {
      console.error(
        `API request failed with status ${res.status}: ${res.statusText}`
      );
      return null;
    }

    const data = await res.json();

    if (
      !data ||
      !data.data ||
      !Array.isArray(data.data) ||
      data.data.length === 0
    ) {
      console.error(
        'Unexpected API response:', JSON.stringify(data, null, 2)
      );
      return null;
    }

    if (!data.data[0].embedding) {
      console.error(
        'No embedding found in response:',
        JSON.stringify(data.data[0], null, 2)
      );
      return null;
    }

    return data.data[0].embedding;
  } catch (error) {
    console.error(
      `Error generating embedding for "${text}":`,
      error.message
    );
    return null;
  }
}
```

Then, use that function to embed all the titles:

```
getting_started_with_vector_search/name_this_book.js
async function embedTitles(books) {
  console.log(`Generating embeddings for all titles...`);

  const promises = books.map((book, i) => {
```

```
  const fullTitle = book.subtitle
    ? `${book.title}: ${book.subtitle}`
    : book.title;

  console.log(` (${i + 1}/${books.length}) ${fullTitle}`);

  return getEmbedding(fullTitle).then(embedding => {
    book.embedding = embedding;
    return book;
  });
});
const booksWithEmbeddings = await Promise.all(promises);

// Filter out books that failed to get embeddings
const validBooks = booksWithEmbeddings.filter(book => book.embedding !== null);

if (validBooks.length < books.length) {
  console.log(`
    Warning:
    ${books.length - validBooks.length} books failed to get embeddings and
    were excluded.
  `);
}

return validBooks;
}
```

This combines the title and subtitle (if present) and generates one embedding per book. All embedding requests are fired off at the same time and processed in parallel. This speeds things up, but if you're working with large datasets or strict API rate limits, you may want to throttle or batch requests instead.

Don't worry if the process still feels mysterious. In the next chapter, we'll unpack exactly how embeddings work and what makes them such a powerful tool for search and recommendation.

Comparing to Your Title Idea

Now you'll embed a new title idea and compare it to the catalog using cosine similarity. Here's how we compute similarity between vectors:

```
getting_started_with_vector_search/name_this_book.js
function cosineSimilarity(a, b) {
  const dot = a.reduce(
    (sum, ai, i) => {
      return sum + ai * b[i];
    },
    0
  );
```

```
  const magA = Math.sqrt(
    a.reduce((sum, ai) => {
      return sum + ai * ai;
    }, 0)
  );
  const magB = Math.sqrt(
    b.reduce((sum, bi) => {
      return sum + bi * bi;
    }, 0)
  );
  return dot / (magA * magB);
}
```

And here's how we find and rank the top matches:

getting_started_with_vector_search/name_this_book.js

```
function compareTitles(queryEmbedding, books) {
  console.log('Comparing against catalog...');
  return books
    .map(book => ({
      ...book,
      similarity: cosineSimilarity(
        book.embedding,
        queryEmbedding
      ),
    }))
    .sort((a, b) => b.similarity - a.similarity)
    .slice(0, 5);
}
```

Putting It All Together

Finally, let's connect everything. This main() function runs the entire flow:
scrape, embed, store, and compare.

getting_started_with_vector_search/name_this_book.js

```
async function main() {
  const DATA_FILE = 'pragprog_titles.json';
  let books;

  if (fs.existsSync(DATA_FILE)) {
    console.log(`Loading cached data from ${DATA_FILE}...`);
    books = JSON.parse(fs.readFileSync(DATA_FILE, 'utf8'));
  } else {
    console.log('No cached data found. Starting fresh.');

    books = await scrapeTitles();
    books = await embedTitles(books);
```

```
  fs.writeFileSync(
    DATA_FILE,
    JSON.stringify(books, null, 2)
  );

  console.log(`Saved ${books.length} books to ${DATA_FILE}`);
}

const query = process.argv.slice(2).join(' ');
if (!query) {
  console.error(
    'Please pass a proposed title as a command-line argument'
  );
  console.error(
    'Example: node name_this_book.js "Mastering Vector Search"'
  );
  process.exit(1);
}

console.log(`\nFinding matches for: "${query}"`);
const queryEmbedding = await getEmbedding(query);
const topMatches = compareTitles(queryEmbedding, books);

console.log(`\nTop matches for "${query}":\n`);
for (const match of topMatches) {
  console.log(
    `- ${match.title}${match.subtitle ? `: ${match.subtitle}` : ''}`
  );
  console.log(
    `   (${(match.similarity * 100).toFixed(2)}% similar)`
  );
  console.log(
    `   ${match.url}\n`
  );
}
}
```

Run the script like this:

```
node name_this_book.js "Vector Search for Everyone"
```

The script will output the top five most similar titles from the catalog along with their similarity scores. A score close to 1 means your title idea is very similar in meaning to a published Pragmatic title, while lower scores indicate less similarity. You can use these results to evaluate whether your idea fits the style and themes of the publisher's catalog. You might also use the output to spark new ideas based on which titles rank highly in similarity.

When you run the script, you'll see the top five matches ranked by similarity. For example, testing the title idea *Learning Vector Search with JavaScript* produced results that leaned into themes of "learning," "programming," and "JavaScript." The closest match, *A Common-Sense Guide to Data Structures and Algorithms in JavaScript*, shared both the language and the educational framing through its use of "learning"-adjacent phrasing. Other top matches included *Machine Learning in Elixir* and *Programming Phoenix LiveView*, which shows that the system focused on action-oriented words like "learning" and "programming" as strong signals. This kind of feedback helps you understand not just which titles are similar but why. Often, they share verbs, technologies, or a how-to tone. You can use that insight to tweak your phrasing or steer your idea toward a more distinctive niche.

Key Takeaways

In this chapter, you used vector search to compare your own book title idea to real titles from the Pragmatic Bookshelf catalog. Along the way, you wrote a complete program that scraped live data, generated embeddings using OpenAI, and ranked results using cosine similarity, all with just a few lines of code. If you haven't already, take a moment to come up with a title idea of your own and plug it into the script to see how it compares.

Let's summarize your major wins:

- You scraped and parsed real book titles from the web.
- You generated vector embeddings with the OpenAI API.
- You compared your title idea to the catalog using cosine similarity.
- You followed the same approach the author used to name this book.

Now that you've seen vector search in action, the next step is to understand how it works.

CHAPTER 2

Understanding Vector Search

In Chapter 1, Getting Started with Vector Search, on page 3, you built a working vector search tool that compared book title ideas using real embeddings and similarity scoring. You got hands-on experience with concepts like vector generation and similarity search, even if you didn't fully understand how they worked yet. This chapter explains the intuition behind vector search and embeddings, including what they are and why they work, without getting into the technical implementation details of generating them. In Chapter 3, Generating Vector Embeddings, on page 15, we'll focus on how to generate embeddings using APIs.

Vector search enhances how applications find and display relevant information by retrieving similar items from large datasets. Unlike traditional search, which matches exact keywords, vector search uses advanced AI models to understand context, meaning, and relationships in data. It works by converting both the content and the search query into dense numerical representations called vectors, which can then be compared for similarity.

What Do Vectors Have to Do with Similarity?

Previously, you generated embeddings for real book titles and compared them using cosine similarity. Each title became a list of numbers, which is a vector, and your proposed title was embedded the same way. Then the script ranked results by how similar those vectors were.

This is all working with what's known as *high-dimensional data*. High-dimensional data means each item is described by many numerical features, sometimes hundreds or even thousands, instead of just two or three.

That's the core idea of vector search: represent things as numbers in a shared space and measure how close they are. But it can feel abstract until you see how those numbers behave.

Let's simplify. Forget high-dimensional space for a minute. Say we're comparing colors. We can describe a color using RGB values of red, green, and blue. These three numbers form a vector. Blue is [0, 0, 255], red is [255, 0, 0], yellow is [255, 255, 0], and so on. If you have a new color, like Slate Blue ([91, 124, 153]), you can compare it to known colors to see what it's closest to.

That's exactly what we did with book titles. The only difference is dimensionality. Instead of 3 numbers like RGB, we worked with 1,536 numbers. But the goal was the same: represent each item as a vector, then find the closest one.

You saw this in action when the title *Learning Vector Search with JavaScript* produced top matches like *A Common-Sense Guide to Data Structures and Algorithms in JavaScript* and *Machine Learning in Elixir*. The system wasn't matching exact words. It was comparing high-dimensional vectors and looking for patterns across hundreds of abstract features. Vectors that pointed in a similar direction were judged to be more alike.

So what creates these vectors? How do we go from raw text to numbers that capture meaning? That's where embeddings come in.

Unpacking the Concept of Embeddings

Text is more complex than colors. You need a way to generate vectors for titles or paragraphs so that two texts with similar meanings produce points that are close together in vector space. One common technique is to create something called an embedding.

An embedding is a long list of numbers. Each number represents a feature extracted by a machine learning model. If you use OpenAI's embedding model, each vector has 1,536 dimensions. You can think of these as axes in a massive coordinate space.

The goal is for texts that mean similar things to have similar embeddings. For example, the phrases "Learning JavaScript" and "Mastering JavaScript" should land near each other in vector space, since they share both subject matter and educational intent. A phrase like "Exploring Ruby" might be close, as well, because it has a similar structure and purpose. But something like "Deploying Kubernetes at Scale" would be much farther away, even though it also describes a technical skill, because it belongs to a completely different domain.

You create an embedding by feeding your text into a pretrained model. That model has already learned how language works by training on massive datasets. It compresses everything it knows into a set of internal weights. When you pass in new text, it produces a vector that captures key aspects of the input. This process may feel like a black box for now, but we'll demystify it step by step.

Understanding Similarity

Once you have embeddings, the next question is how to compare them. In other words, how can you tell which vectors are close to each other?

To compare embeddings, we need a way to measure how similar two vectors are. The most common methods are cosine similarity, which measures the angle between vectors (regardless of their size) and dot product, which considers both their direction and magnitude. Cosine similarity answers "are these vectors pointing the same way?" while dot product adds the question, "and how strong is that signal?"

To make it more tangible, imagine comparing fruit. Let's say we use made-up 3D embeddings to represent "apple," "banana," and "orange." These numbers might reflect how sweet, fibrous, or acidic each fruit is. If the vectors are close, we assume the fruits are similar.

In fact, let's calculate it.

```
understanding_vector_search/similarity_applies_bananas_oranges.js
const vectors = {
  Apple: [0.9, 0.1, 0.0],
  Banana: [0.7, 0.3, 0.0],
  Orange: [0.8, 0.2, 0.1],
};

/**
 * Calculate the dot product of two vectors.
 * @param {Array<number>} vec1 - First vector.
 * @param {Array<number>} vec2 - Second vector.
 * @returns {number} - Dot product of the two vectors.
 */
const calculateDotProduct = (vec1, vec2) =>
  vec1.reduce((sum, value, index) => sum + value * vec2[index], 0);

/**
 * Calculate the magnitude of a vector.
 * @param {Array<number>} vec - The vector.
 * @returns {number} - Magnitude of the vector.
 */
```

```
const calculateMagnitude = (vec) =>
  Math.sqrt(vec.reduce((sum, value) => sum + value ** 2, 0));
/**
 * Calculate the cosine similarity between two vectors.
 * @param {Array<number>} vec1 - First vector.
 * @param {Array<number>} vec2 - Second vector.
 * @returns {number} - Cosine similarity.
 */
const calculateCosineSimilarity = (vec1, vec2) => {
  const dotProduct = calculateDotProduct(vec1, vec2);
  const magnitude1 = calculateMagnitude(vec1);
  const magnitude2 = calculateMagnitude(vec2);
  return dotProduct / (magnitude1 * magnitude2);
};

// Example: Calculate cosine similarity between "Apple" and "Banana"
const apple = vectors.Apple;
const banana = vectors.Banana;

const similarity = calculateCosineSimilarity(apple, banana);

console.log(`Apple/Banana similarity: ${similarity.toFixed(3)}`);
```

This code calculates the cosine similarity between "apple" and "banana." Even though the numbers are arbitrary, the math shows how closely aligned the vectors are. That alignment becomes the basis for comparison in vector search.

Key Takeaways

In this chapter, you learned that a vector is just a list of numbers and that similarity between vectors can be measured with cosine similarity or dot product. You saw how embeddings represent complex data as vectors and how systems use those vectors to find the most relevant matches.

These ideas might feel new now, but you've already used them. The title-matching script in Chapter 1 embedded and compared titles using these exact principles. With a better understanding of what was going on under the hood, you're now ready to go deeper.

In the next chapter, we'll explore how embeddings are generated, what makes a good embedding, and why these representations are so powerful for building intelligent search systems.

CHAPTER 3

Generating Vector Embeddings

You now understand how embeddings represent meaning in vector form and how they're used in similarity calculations. In this chapter, you'll learn how to generate those embeddings using the OpenAI API. We'll walk through what the API offers, how to use it in code, and how to interpret the results.

Breaking Down an Individual Embedding

Embeddings are dense vector representations of data that capture the relationships between different entities. We use embeddings to represent data, making performing operations such as similarity calculations easier. The embeddings capture both the semantic and syntactic relationships between entities. For example, in the case of words, embeddings can capture relationships such as *king* is to *queen*, which is a semantic relationship, and *king* is to *kings*, which is a syntactic relationship.

What does that look like in reality? Let's take the king and queen example and show how we represent them as embeddings. In the case of word embeddings, the word *king* might be represented as a vector embedding that looks like this:

```
[
  0.010183674,
  -0.003974117,
  0.0073341774,
  -0.011770561,
  -0.031903327,
  0.018601075,
  -0.014723551,
  -0.03132377,
  ...
]
```

Why did I include an ellipsis at the end of the vector? Because the vector is much longer than what I've shown here! That's because, depending on the model that generates the embeddings, the vector can be of different lengths and are usually long.

Did You Know? Embeddings and Language

Embeddings are widely used in natural language processing (NLP) to represent words and phrases in a way that captures their meaning. This helps with challenges like polysemy, which are words like *dive* with multiple meanings depending on context. Embeddings disambiguate based on usage.

They also outperform techniques like stemming (reducing *jogging, jogged, jogs* to *jog*) and lemmatization (reducing *ran, running, runs* to *run*). Rather than relying on rules, embeddings capture these relationships naturally by learning from context.

In this instance, the model that generated the word *king* embedding was text-embedding-ada-002 from OpenAI.[1] The embeddings created by this model have *1,536 dimensions*. The number of dimensions means that the vector is a list of 1,536 values, each representing a different aspect of the word *king*. In Chapter 9, Incorporating Vector Search Functionality, on page 87, we explore optimizing the embedding results by reducing the vectors' dimensionality. Vector dimensionality reduction is a complex subject since it involves a trade-off between the quality of the embeddings and the computational resources required to generate them. Yet, it can impact your overall performance and cost efficiency.

The values represented by each of those floating point numbers represent a different semantic and syntactic aspect of the word *king*. The model that generated the embeddings has learned to represent the word *king* in a way that captures its relationships with other words. As we said above, this means *king* and *queen* will be close together in the vector space, while *king* and *apple* will be farther apart.

Did You Know? Embedding vs. Generative Models

Embedding models (like OpenAI's Ada) create dense vector representations of data, capturing semantic relationships that are beneficial for search or recommendations. In contrast, generative models (like GPT) produce content—such as text, images, or audio. Both use transformers, but embedding models focus on contextual vector creation, whereas generative models generate coherent content sequentially.

---

1.   https://platform.openai.com/docs/guides/embeddings

Generating Embeddings with the OpenAI API

You're now ready to take your first step into working with vector search. Over the past several chapters, you've explored the concepts behind vectors, vector embeddings, generative and embedding models, and more. All this knowledge has equipped you to begin developing your first application of vector search. In software development, we aim to make things understandable, not mysterious. That's why we've spent this time building your understanding so you can build confidence.

As mentioned earlier, we'll use the OpenAI Embeddings API to generate embeddings. The OpenAI Embeddings API is a powerful tool that allows you to generate embeddings for text, images, and more. The API is easy to use and well-documented, making it an excellent choice for developers new to working with embeddings. In this section, we'll learn how to generate embeddings using the OpenAI API. We'll explore the various options available in the API and how to work with them to create embeddings for your data.

OpenAI maintains an official SDK for Node.js,[2] which incorporates the functionality of the OpenAI APIs, including the Embeddings API. You install the SDK with npm, the Node.js package manager, by running the following command:

```
npm install openai
```

In addition to using the SDK, you can also make an API call directly using cURL. The OpenAI documentation[3] provides code snippets in cURL, Node.js, and Python for all of the relevant examples. We'll use those code examples in this book wherever appropriate.

Whether using the SDK or making an API call using cURL, you'll still need an API key to authenticate your requests. You can obtain an API key by signing up for an account on the OpenAI platform.[4] Once you have an API key, you can use it to authenticate your requests and access the OpenAI APIs. For the cURL request, you'll need to include the API key in the request header. For the Node.js SDK, you'll provide the API key when instantiating a new instance of the OpenAI client.

Here's an example request in cURL taken from the official documentation; we'll look at each of the parameters in detail:

---

2. https://github.com/openai/openai-node
3. https://platform.openai.com/docs/guides/embeddings/what-are-embeddings
4. https://platform.openai.com/docs/overview

```
curl https://api.openai.com/v1/embeddings \
  -H "Content-Type: application/json" \
  -H "Authorization: Bearer $OPENAI_API_KEY" \
  -d '{
    "input": "Your text string goes here",
    "model": "text-embedding-3-small"
  }'
```

First, we see the API endpoint's URL, https://api.openai.com/v1/embeddings. Next, we see the headers in the request. The Content-Type header specifies that the request body is JSON. The Authorization header consists of the API key used to authenticate the request. Finally, we see the request body, which includes the input text and the model for generating the embeddings. In this case, the input text is "Your text string goes here", and the model is "text-embedding-3-small".

The list of available models can also be found in the documentation,[5] and new models are introduced from time to time while existing models are updated. In effect, the two parameters we need to provide, whether in a cURL request or the SDK, are input and model. That same request would look like the following using the SDK:

```
basics_of_vector_embeddings/first_api_request.js
const main = async () => {
  try {
    const embedding = await openai.embeddings.create({
      model: "text-embedding-ada-002",
      input: "Your text string goes here",
      encoding_format: "float",
    });

    console.log(embedding.data[0].embedding);
    console.log("Model used:", embedding.model);
    console.log("Tokens consumed:", embedding.usage.total_tokens);
  } catch (error) {
    console.error("Error generating embedding:", error);
  }
};

main();
```

Did you notice the additional encoding_format parameter in the request created with the SDK? This parameter is one of two main ones you can use to fine-tune your request to fit your needs. Let's explore them:

- encoding_format: Decide what format you want the data returned in, either as floating point numbers or base64 encoded. The default is float, but base64 offers advantages if you prioritize compatibility and portability.

---

5.   https://platform.openai.com/docs/guides/embeddings/embedding-models

Base64 data can further compress the data if storage is a significant constraint, and many communications protocols handle base64 encoded data more easily.

- *Dimensions*: Here, you get to specify how many dimensions you want your output to be. This feature is only supported, as of the time of this writing, for the text-embedding-3 model from OpenAI. The more dimensionality an embedding has, the more context it has—both semantic and syntactic—but it also means the more space it takes up. Figuring out the right balance for your data involves fine-tuning to achieve the optional dimensionality. In many instances, it's safer to use the default provided by the model.

Once you've submitted your request, the API returns the data in the following format:

```
basics_of_vector_embeddings/embedding_api_example_response.json
{
  "object": "list",
  "data": [
    {
      "object": "embedding",
      "embedding": [
        0.0023064255,
        -0.009327292,
        -0.0028842222
      ],
      "index": 0
    }
  ],
  "model": "text-embedding-ada-002",
  "usage": {
    "prompt_tokens": 8,
    "total_tokens": 8
  }
}
```

The API returns the actual embedding inside the data array, nested within the embedding object. In addition to the embedding, you receive information on the model you used and the total number of tokens created to generate the embedding. Tokens are how the language model breaks down text into smaller units for processing; they represent chunks of text, as we explained earlier, that the model uses to compute embeddings. Understanding the number of tokens consumed is important because APIs often charge based on token usage, so monitoring token counts helps you manage costs and optimize your application's performance.

Now that we've walked through using the API with the Node.js SDK and explored the response from the API, why don't you send your first request?

Create a new file called request.js and add the following, replacing the "Your text string goes here" in the input parameter with whatever you wish to turn into a vector embedding:

```
basics_of_vector_embeddings/first_api_request.js
import OpenAI from "openai";
import dotenv from "dotenv";

dotenv.config();

const openai = new OpenAI({
  apiKey: process.env.OPENAI_API_KEY,
});

const main = async () => {
  try {
    const embedding = await openai.embeddings.create({
      model: "text-embedding-ada-002",
      input: "Your text string goes here",
      encoding_format: "float",
    });

    console.log(embedding.data[0].embedding);
    console.log("Model used:", embedding.model);
    console.log("Tokens consumed:", embedding.usage.total_tokens);
  } catch (error) {
    console.error("Error generating embedding:", error);
  }
};

main();
```

Create a .env file in the root folder alongside the file and add the following environment variable, replacing the your-api-key-here value with your actual OpenAI API key:

```
OPENAI_API_KEY=your-api-key-here
```

Remember, *do not* commit your environment variables to any public code repository, such as GitHub. If you're adding your code to GitHub, make sure to include the .env file in the list of files to ignore in your .gitignore file.

Then run the script from your command line using node by executing the following:

```
node first_api_request.js
```

Once you've done so, you should see the new vector embedding outputted in your terminal, information on the model you used, and the number of tokens consumed.

That's it! You've just sent your first request and received your first vector embedding back in response! Congratulations. You're now ready to begin implementing vector search in an application.

Key Takeaways

In this chapter, we explored vector embeddings, how they are generated, and why they're essential to modern applications such as search and recommendation systems. We discussed different types of embedding models and compared them to generative models. We concluded with a hands-on walkthrough of generating embeddings using the OpenAI Embeddings API.

These are the key takeaways from this chapter:

- Vector embeddings represent data (such as text) as dense vectors in high-dimensional space, capturing semantic and syntactic relationships.

- Embedding models like OpenAI's Ada can be used to create these vectors from plain text using APIs.

- Embeddings are foundational to systems like search and recommendation engines.

- You now know how to generate embeddings using the OpenAI Embeddings API.

The next chapter will focus on setting up our development environment, including scaffolding our application and configuring a vector database to hold our vector embeddings.

Part II

Building a Vector Search Service

CHAPTER 4

Building the Foundation for Vector Search

In the last few chapters, you've explored the fundamentals of vector search, from embeddings and embedding models to neural networks and NLP concepts. Along the way, you created vector embeddings. Now it's time to shift from theory to practice. From here on out, we'll focus on building a real-world application powered by vector search.

In the coming chapters, you'll gain real experience integrating vector search into your application. We'll cover all aspects of building from the ground up. We'll start with setting up your development environment, learning about the different developer tooling we'll be using, and configuring a vector database to store the embeddings that will power the search in your application.

Ready to get started? Let's get going!

Scaffolding Your Node.js Project

Before we dive into scaffolding, it's helpful to understand the project you'll be building throughout this book. As we discussed in Chapter 2, Understanding Vector Search, on page 11, vector search can have many practical use cases, from anomaly detection to content recommendation engines to similarity search. You'll be creating a fully featured blog platform that uses vector search to respond to user queries. Instead of relying on exact keyword matches, the search bar will return results based on how closely a query semantically aligns with blog post content that will help users discover relevant material even when they don't know the right keywords.

Now that you know what you're building, let's set the foundation.

Scaffolding involves creating the necessary directories and files, installing dependencies, and configuring essential settings.

We won't be building the blog platform from scratch, though! Instead, we'll be taking advantage of the RealWorld Example Apps[1] project, which aims to create fully functioning example applications in as many different programming languages and frameworks as possible. The RealWorld Example Apps project provides a fully featured blog platform that includes user authentication, article creation, article editing, article deletion, and article search functionality. The creators of the RealWorld project call these blog platforms *Conduit* and you can find all the implementations the community has already created[2] sorted by front-end, back-end, and full-stack versions.

If you ever get stuck at any stage of the book, you can always find the code for the entire project we'll be building on GitHub.[3] At various stages of the process, we'll refer back to the codebase, so you don't even need to bookmark this page.

The first step in creating the scaffolding for our Node.js project is to create the necessary directories and files. We'll start by creating a new directory for our project and then creating the necessary subdirectories within that directory. We'll need the following directories, starting with the root-level directory for our project, which you can name whatever you like, perhaps vector-blog-platform.

We'll begin by setting up the back end of our blog platform as an API service. To do that, we'll organize our project into a clear directory structure that separates concerns like data storage, embedding logic, and routing. This layout makes it easier to expand the app in the future, including adding a front end that you can either build yourself or copy from the GitHub repository.

Go ahead and create the following directories in the root directory of your project:

- api/: Contains the core API logic and configuration for the back end, including security and database connectivity.

- config/: Contains the configuration files for the back end, including environment variables and database connection settings.

- controllers/: Contains the controller files, which handle requests and responses for various routes.

---

1. https://github.com/gothinkster/realworld
2. https://codebase.show/projects/realworld
3. https://github.com/hummusonrails/vector-example-blog-platform

- middleware/: Contains custom middleware logic, such as authentication and JWT verification.

- models/: Contains the model files, which define the structure of the data stored in the database.

- routes/: Contains route definitions for different endpoints in the application.

- views/: Contains the default view rendered by the server if the API service is accessed via a web browser.

When you've created all these folders, your folder structure should look like the following:

```
vector-blog-platform/
├── api/
├── config/
├── controllers/
├── middleware/
├── models/
├── routes/
├── views/
```

You've now created the basic folder structure for the project. Throughout the book, we'll be adding files and directories to this structure as we build out the functionality of the blog platform. The next steps are to install the necessary dependencies for the project and configure the vector database that will store the embeddings for the blog posts.

Before we move on to installing dependencies, it's a good time to discuss the importance of database specialization for vector embeddings and vector search. The special nature of vectors means we need to think carefully about efficient storage for them that can also provide us with fast querying abilities. In the next section, we'll discuss the considerations you should take into account when choosing a database for your project.

Choosing a Vector Database

You may look at this section title and think to yourself, "Why do I need a special database for vector embeddings? Can't I just use any database?" In the example project we'll be building, we need a database that can handle "regular" data—that is, the data that is not vector embeddings, like the blog content, user profiles, and similar information, and we also need a database that can store, index, and query vector embeddings efficiently. We could separate out those concerns, but our intention is to not introduce any additional complexity and to reduce the sprawl of our database infrastructure.

So we need a database that can handle diverse types of data, including structured, unstructured, and semi-structured data.

Vector embeddings are unstructured data, and they're also high-dimensional. As we discussed in Chapter 2, Understanding Vector Search, on page 11, high-dimensional means that the embedding has many features to describe the data. The OpenAI Ada embedding model has 1,536 dimensions, which means each embedding is a list of 1,536 values. This is a lot of data to store and query, especially when you consider that we'll be storing embeddings for every blog post and user query! As a result, we also need a database that efficiently handles high-dimensional data.

Optimizing for performance translates to also having the ability to properly index the vector embedding data. Indexing vector embeddings means creating a data structure that allows for fast retrieval of vectors based on their similarity to a query vector. Unlike traditional indexing, which might rely on exact matches (like keyword search, as we explained in Chapter 3, Generating Vector Embeddings, on page 15), vector indexing is focused on similarity search, which is to say finding vectors that are closest to the query in high-dimensional space.

We will discuss in detail the mechanics of, and setting up, vector search indexes in Chapter 7, Creating a Vector Search Service, on page 63, but for now, it's important to understand that the database we choose must be able to handle indexing vector embeddings efficiently. The database must be able to create and update indexes quickly, and it must be able to query the indexes to return results in a timely manner.

Now that we have a better understanding of the requirements for our database, let's take a look at the different types of databases that are available for storing and querying vector embeddings:

- *Document databases* are databases that store data in a document format, such as JSON or XML. Document databases are well suited for storing unstructured data, such as vector embeddings, as they do not require a predefined schema. Document databases can be optimized for querying and indexing high-dimensional data, making them a good choice for storing vector embeddings.

- *Graph databases* are databases that store data in a graph format, with nodes representing entities and edges representing relationships between entities. Graph databases are well suited for storing and querying complex relationships between data, such as the relationships between vector embeddings. Graph databases can also optimize querying and indexing of high-dimensional data, making them another good choice for storing vector embeddings.

- *SQL databases* are relational databases that store data in tables with rows and columns. SQL databases are well suited for storing structured data, such as user profiles and blog content, but they can also be used to store vector embeddings. While perhaps not the most conventional path to take, they're nonetheless capable of storing and querying vector embeddings.

> ## Other Database Options
>
> Many options are available for deploying a database in any one of these three categories. What follows is a thoroughly non-exhaustive list of databases that you could consider for your project, organized by type of database:
>
> - *Document databases*: MongoDB, Pinecone
> - *Graph databases*: Neo4j, TigerGraph
> - *SQL databases*: Supabase, Neon
>
> Each option provides multiple deployment methods, pricing structures, and feature sets, including managed and self-hosted solutions. While a full comparison is beyond our scope, I encourage you to explore and select the best fit for your needs and budget.

For the purposes of this book, we'll be using Couchbase as our database of choice. Couchbase optimizes the storage and querying of high-dimensional data, making it well suited for storing vector embeddings. It also offers Capella,[4] a fully managed cloud service with one-click deployment to AWS, Google Cloud, or Azure. In addition to its technical capabilities, Capella provides a generous free tier, which is ideal for experimentation and learning in a project like this.

We're using a document database, specifically a JSON document database, because it allows us to work with flexible, semi-structured data. JSON (JavaScript Object Notation) is a lightweight and human-readable format for storing data as key-value pairs. It's widely used in web development and works naturally with JavaScript-based tools. The document model makes it easy to store and query a variety of data types, including vector embeddings, blog posts, and user profiles, all in a format that aligns well with the structure of the application we're building.

---

4.   https://cloud.couchbase.com

The next step in setting up your Node.js project is to install the necessary dependencies. Dependencies are external libraries or packages that your project relies on to function correctly.

Installing Dependencies

In this section, we'll install the dependencies for our Node.js project, including the libraries and tools we will use to interact with the vector database and generate and store the embeddings for the blog posts.

To install dependencies in our project, we need a package.json file at the root level of the project. The package.json file is a manifest file that contains metadata about the project, including the project name, version, description, and dependencies. It's the primary file that npm uses to install packages and manage dependencies for the project.

Thankfully, npm provides a command to generate a package.json file for you. To generate a package.json file, run the following command in the root directory of your project:

```
npm init -y
```

The -y flag tells npm to use the default values for the prompts that normally appear when you run the npm init command. At the conclusion of the command, it will output the structure of your package.json file to your terminal. It should be similar to the following:

building_the_foundation_for_vector_search/example_package_json.json
```
{
  "name": "vector-blog-platform",
  "version": "1.0.0",
  "description": "",
  "main": "index.js",
  "scripts": {
    "test": "echo \"Error: no test specified\" && exit 1"
  },
  "keywords": [],
  "author": "",
  "license": "ISC",
  "dependencies": {
    "ottoman": "^2.5.1",
    "openai": "^4.96.2",
    "dotenv": "^16.5.0"
  }
}
```

Now that we have a package.json file, we can start installing the dependencies for our project. We're making great progress! At this point, we could just list the dependencies to install, but then you would be simply "copying and pasting" without understanding what you're installing. Let's take a moment to understand the dependencies we'll be installing and why we need them.

We need to consider three areas of application development when installing dependencies. The database is one area and, as we discussed earlier, we cannot use just any database, but rather we need a database that can store, index, and query vector embeddings. We'll be building using an ORM, or Object Relational Mapping library, to interact with the database. An ORM is a programming construct that enables us to interact with data in a database using objects like an object-oriented programming language. It might be easier to understand with a practical example.

Most of the libraries we're using in this project, including the OpenAI SDK and Ottoman, perform asynchronous operations. These operations take time—like querying a database or making a network request—and would normally block the program from continuing. To handle this, we'll be using JavaScript's async/await syntax. async/await allows us to write asynchronous code that looks and behaves more like regular, synchronous code, making it easier to read and maintain. You'll see this pattern throughout the book whenever we fetch data, store embeddings, or interact with external APIs.

Let's say your application has users, and the model for a user might look like this:

building_the_foundation_for_vector_search/example_user_model.json

```
{
    "id": 1,
    "name": "John Doe",
    "email": "john.doe@not_a_real_email.com",
    "password": "hashed_password",
    "created_at": "2024-01-01T00:00:00Z",
    "updated_at": "2024-05-01T00:00:00Z"
}
```

If you're working with a relational database, you'd have a User table in your database that would parallel the structure of a user, whereas if you're working with a document database, you'd have user documents, one for each user, that would likewise parallel the structure of a user. Now, this is where the benefit of an ORM comes in. The focus of this book is not about ORMs, but we need to take a moment together to understand how an ORM can simplify the process of interacting with databases, regardless of the type of database you're using.

In the example of the User model, you'd have somewhere in your codebase a User class that would look something like this:

```javascript
building_the_foundation_for_vector_search/example_user_class.js
class User {
  constructor(id, name, email, password, created_at, updated_at) {
    this.id = id;
    this.name = name;
    this.email = email;
    this.password = password;
    this.created_at = created_at;
    this.updated_at = updated_at;
  }
}

export default User;
```

The User class represents a user record in your database. You can create a new User object, set its properties, and save it to the database. The ORM library handles translating the object into a database query. This is a high-level overview of how an ORM works and why it can be helpful in application development.

One of the biggest advantages of using an ORM is how it simplifies querying data. Rather than writing raw queries or complex database calls, an ORM, like Ottoman, lets you use familiar JavaScript methods and chaining to express what you're looking for. This is especially helpful when querying nested or hierarchical data common in JSON document databases. For example, finding all blog posts with a certain tag or retrieving user records based on a similarity score can be done using intuitive methods like Model.find() with filter conditions, which Ottoman translates into optimized queries behind the scenes. This not only improves readability but also reduces the risk of writing inefficient or incorrect queries.

The second key step is transforming blog content into vector embeddings, allowing us to perform similarity searches. We'll also transform users' queries into vector embeddings to search the content. The generation of a new embedding for every query needs to happen quickly, so we'll need to consider performance and make sure that the process takes as little time as possible. Recent research into user behavior shows that 40 percent of users will leave a website if a response takes more than *three seconds* to load.[5] That's a lot of pressure, so we need to ensure the platform we choose and the SDK we build with can handle the load.

5.　https://www.forbes.com/advisor/business/software/website-statistics/

The transformation of the content into embeddings can happen at the time of content creation, so we'll also need to establish criteria for when to update embeddings as authors add new content. For example, does every edit warrant a revised embedding? Or only certain edits? These are questions we'll need to answer as we build out the functionality of the blog platform. For now, it's safe to say that a single typo correction probably shouldn't trigger a new embedding generation. Or should it? We'll leave that for later on as we discuss optimizing search results and other more advanced topics.

The last application management area we'll rely on is environment variables. Environment variables are set outside your application to configure it at runtime. They store sensitive data, such as API keys or database connection strings, keeping this information out of your codebase. Using environment variables makes your application secure and easily configurable across different environments.

I would be remiss if I didn't mention the obligatory security warning. When working with environment variables, it's important that you do not commit sensitive information to your version control system. Always add your environment variables to a .env file and include that file in your .gitignore to prevent it from being committed. This will help keep your sensitive information secure during development.

For production environments, however, storing secrets in a .env file is not recommended. Instead, use a secure method such as injecting environment variables from a secrets manager at runtime or reading them from a mounted secrets location provided by your cloud platform or container orchestration system. This adds an extra layer of protection and ensures your secrets are handled safely in production.

With that background on the why and what of our dependencies, let's specify the dependencies we'll be installing for our project. We'll be using the following libraries and tools to build our blog platform:

- *Ottoman.js:*[6] A Node.js ORM library (to be more precise, an ODM library since we are working with JSON documents for our data and not a relational model) for Couchbase that will allow us to interact with the Couchbase database using objects.

---

6.   https://ottomanjs.com/

- *OpenAI Node.js SDK:*[7] The official Node.js SDK for the OpenAI API that will allow us to generate vector embeddings for the content and user queries in our blog platform.

- *dotenv:*[8] A zero-dependency module that loads environment variables from a .env file into process.env to keep our sensitive information secure.

To install these three dependencies, you can run the following command in the root directory of your project:

```
npm install ottoman openai dotenv
```

You can verify that npm installed the dependencies correctly by checking the package.json file or by running the following command:

```
npm list
```

Upon running npm list, you'll see an output similar to this one:

```
vector-blog-platform@1.0.0 /path/to/your/project
├── dotenv@16.4.5
├── openai@4.58.2
└── ottoman@2.5.0
```

This output shows the dependencies were installed successfully and are now available for use in your project. With the dependencies installed, you are now ready to start building out the functionality of your blog platform!

Key Takeaways

In this chapter, you laid the groundwork for building a vector search application by setting up your development environment and preparing the tools and structure needed to support vector embedding workflows.

Here's a quick summary of what you've accomplished so far and what to carry forward as we begin implementing vector search in your application:

- You set up your development environment by installing Node.js, scaffolding your project structure, and selecting a suitable vector database.

- You learned that vector embeddings are unstructured, high-dimensional data that require specialized indexing to enable fast and accurate search.

- You explored the types of databases that can store vector data, including document, graph, and relational databases, and understood why document databases are a strong fit.

---

7. https://github.com/openai/openai-node
8. https://www.npmjs.com/package/dotenv

- You installed and configured core dependencies, including an ORM (Ottoman), the OpenAI SDK for embedding generation, and dotenv for environment variable management.

In the next chapter, we'll begin implementing the search functionality in our Node.js application. We'll cover how to query our vector database for similar embeddings and return relevant results to the user.

CHAPTER 5

Structuring the Back End for Vector Search

It's time to implement one of the core features of vector search. In earlier chapters, we discussed how embeddings represent documents in a high-dimensional space and allow us to compare meaning across content. Now let's start writing real application code to support that functionality.

We'll extend the Real World Project,[1] an open source Medium.com clone with an existing API spec. The project already includes user accounts, posts, tags, and comments. You'll build on top of that by adding vector search to power more relevant content discovery.

You're at a key point in your vector search journey. Let's get started!

Introduction to the Back-End Architecture

To support vector embeddings and search, we'll add a new services/ folder to the existing back-end structure. This is where we'll place logic for calling external APIs, such as OpenAI's embedding endpoint, and for running similarity queries.

This keeps embedding logic separate from routes and controllers, aligning with back-end best practices. Here's what the updated folder structure looks like:

```
vector-blog-platform/
├── api/
├── config/
├── controllers/
├── middleware/
├── models/
├── routes/
├── services/ # New folder
├── views/
```

---

1. https://github.com/gothinkster/realworld

If you want to explore or follow along with the full codebase, you can find it on GitHub.[2]

Creating Data Models for the Platform

A lot of times when I'm excited to build something new, I jump straight into coding. Later, after more rewrites than I'd like to admit, I realize I should have planned the data structure first.

Perhaps this can be best expressed with some Latin:

> *Carpe datum*—Seize the data!

Alternatively, one could look back to one of the classic sets of "Rules" of programming authored by Rob Pike in his 1989 paper, "Notes on Programming in C":[3]

Rule 5. Data dominates. If you've chosen the right data structures and organized things well, the algorithms will almost always be self-evident. Data structures, not algorithms, are central to programming.

In that spirit, before building the vector embedding service and committing code, we'll take a moment to model the data. Thoughtful data modeling is key to enabling meaningful vector operations later. While this project includes standard models for users, articles, tags, and comments, we'll only venture into the ones most relevant to vector search.

In the blog platform we're building, we'll have the following entities:

- Users
- Articles
- Tags
- Comments

Each of these entities will have specific attributes that define them and their relationships with other entities. Let's take a look at the Article model, the one most associated with the vector search functionality for the platform.

Defining the Article Model

The Article model will represent the blog posts on the platform. Users will be able to create articles, add tags to articles, and comment on articles. The Article model will store information about each article, such as the title, body, author, tags, and comments. The Article model will also establish relationships

---

2.   https://github.com/hummusonrails/vector-example-blog-platform
3.   http://www.catb.org/esr/writings/taoup/html/ch01s06.html#rule5

with the user entity, as each article will have an author, and with the tag entity, as each article can have multiple tags.

The Article model will have the following attributes:

- id: A unique identifier for the article.
- slug: A unique slug for the article, derived from the title.
- title: The title of the article.
- description: A short description or summary of the article.
- body: The body or content of the article.
- author: The user ID of the author of the article.
- tagList: An array of tag IDs for tags associated with the article.
- comments: An array of comment IDs for comments on the article.
- favoritesCount: The number of users who have selected the article as a favorite.

Looking at the author attribute, we can see that it's a user ID, establishing a relationship between the article entity and the user entity. The comments attribute is an array of comment IDs, establishing a relationship between the article entity and the comment entity. Similarly, the tagList attribute is an array of tag IDs, establishing a relationship between the article entity and the tag entity. As we did when describing the User model, let's visualize the Article model and its relationships to further understand the data model:

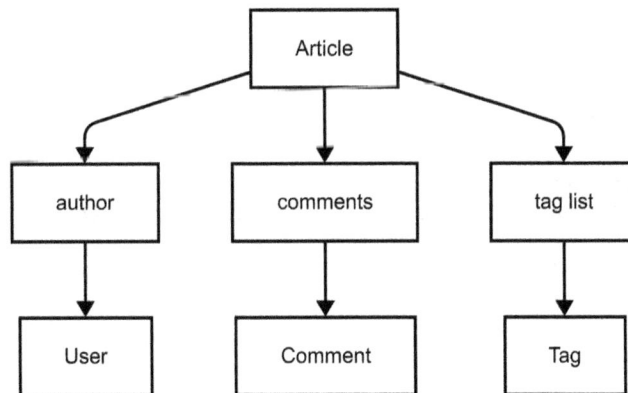

Now that we have a good understanding of the data model for the article entity, let's write the code using Ottoman.js to define the Article model. Create a new file called Article.js in the models/ folder and import the necessary dependencies:

implementing_vector_generation_service/create_article_model.js

```
import { Schema, model, getModel } from 'ottoman';
import slugify from 'slugify';
```

In the preceding code, we're importing functions and modules from Ottoman.js, a JavaScript library, to help us interact with our database from our models, namely the Schema, model, and getModel functions. You'll also notice a unique import for the Article model, which is the slugify library.[4] This library will help us generate unique slugs for the articles based on the title. All of these imports are part of a couchbaseClient that we'll create at the end of this chapter.

Next, let's define the schema for the Article model using the syntax from Ottoman.js:

```
implementing_vector_generation_service/create_article_model.js
const articleSchema = new Schema({
  slug: {
    type: String,
    unique: true,
    lowercase: true,
    index: true,
  },
  title: {
    type: String,
    required: true,
  },
  description: {
    type: String,
    required: true,
  },
  body: {
    type: String,
    required: true,
  },
  // Creates an array of tags, defaulting to an empty array
  // `() => []` is used instead of [] to avoid shared references
  tagList: {
    type: [{ type: String, ref: 'Tag' }],
    default: () => [],
  },
  author: {
    type: String,
    ref: 'User',
  },
  favoritesCount: {
    type: Number,
    default: 0,
  },
```

---

4.   https://www.npmjs.com/package/slugify

```
    // Comments are stored as an array of references to Comment documents
    // Again, default is a function to return a fresh array per instance
    comments: {
      type: [{ type: String, ref: 'Comment' }],
      default: () => [],
    },

    embedding: {
      type: [Number],
      default: () => [],
    },
  },
  {
    timestamps: true,
  });

// Before saving updates, regenerate the slug based on the new title
// This ensures the slug stays in sync when the title changes
articleSchema.pre('update', function (document) {
  document.slug = slugify(document.title, {
    lower: true,
    replacement: '-',
  });
});


// Converts the article instance to a response object for API output,
// including author profile and favorited status
articleSchema.methods.toArticleResponse = async function (user) {
  const User = getModel('User');
  const authorObj = await User.findById(this.author);
  return {
    slug: this.slug,
    articleSlug: this.slug,
    title: this.title,
    description: this.description,
    body: this.body,
    createdAt: this.createdAt,
    updatedAt: this.updatedAt,
    tagList: this.tagList,
    favorited: user ? user.isFavorite(this.id) : false,
    favoritesCount: this.favoritesCount,
    author: authorObj.toProfileJSON(user)
  };
};


// Adds a comment reference to the article's comments array,
// if not already present
articleSchema.methods.addComment = async function (commentId) {
  if (this.comments.indexOf(commentId) === -1) {
    this.comments.push(commentId);
  }
```

```
  return this.save();
};

// Removes a comment reference from the article's comments array,
// if present
articleSchema.methods.removeComment = async function (commentId) {
  const idx = this.comments.indexOf(commentId);
  if (idx !== -1) {
    this.comments.splice(idx, 1);
  }
  return this.save();
};
const scope = process.env.DB_SCOPE || "_default";
const Article = model('Article', articleSchema, { scopeName: scope });

export { articleSchema, Article };
```

The model defines the attributes we discussed earlier for articles. The slug, title, description, and body attributes are required fields, with the slug field being unique and indexed for faster search performance. The tagList field is an array of tag IDs, establishing relationships between the article entity and the tag entity. The author field is a user ID, establishing a relationship between the article entity and the user entity. The comments field is an array of comment IDs, establishing a relationship between the article entity and the comment entity. The favoritesCount field is a number that tracks the number of users who have selected the article as a favorite.

You'll also notice the embedding field, which is an array of numbers. This field will store the vector embedding for the article, which we'll generate and store in the database. This field will be critical for performing similarity searches based on the vector embeddings.

We also use a pre hook to automatically generate a clean slug from the title, using the slugify library. Let's now take a brief look at the other models and their role in the platform. They have less of a role in creating the vector search functionality, but understanding how they work on a high-level will be helpful in moving forward.

Defining the Other Models

As mentioned near the start of this chapter, the blog platform holds models for users, articles, comments and tags. The Article model is the centerpiece of the vector search process, as it will hold the vector embeddings the platform creates. The rest of the models are vital to the platform but not as relevant to the focus of our exploration. Here's a brief overview of each of the other models. The full code for each model can be found at the GitHub repository for the project.

- The User model can author articles, follow other users, and favorite articles. These relationships may later help personalize vector search results if you wish to extend the functionality you've learned in this book to create filters to search by followed users' articles or favorited articles.

- Comments are associated with articles and written by users. While they're not directly embedded or indexed for vector search, they add contextual richness that could later be used in further enhancements with hybrid search strategies.

- Tags are used to categorize articles and support basic filtering. Since we won't generate or store vector embeddings for tags, we don't need to expand upon them further here.

With this high-level understanding of the supporting models in place, we can now shift our focus back to preparing the back end to generate and persist vector embeddings where they matter most—in the articles themselves.

Connecting Articles to the Database

To generate and store embeddings, we need a back end that can persist data reliably and respond to embedding service calls efficiently. In our case, we're using Couchbase as the underlying database and Ottoman.js as the ODM (Object Document Mapper) to interact with it.

Ottoman makes it easy to model documents in JavaScript and handle relationships between entities like users, articles, and tags. But before we can use it in our models or service logic, we need to configure a shared connection instance to the Couchbase cluster.

Let's set that up now.

Create a new file called couchbaseClient.js in a new subfolder named clients inside the services/ directory. This file will hold our shared Couchbase connection logic and expose a configured Ottoman instance that other parts of the app can reuse.

Your directory should look like this:

```
vector-blog-platform/
├── services/
│   └── clients/
│       └── couchbaseClient.js
```

In that file, add the following code:

```
implementing_vector_generation_service/create_db_connection.js
import {
  connect as connectOttoman,
  start as startOttoman
} from 'ottoman';
import couchbase from 'couchbase';

let clusterInstance;

const connectToCouchbase = async () => {
  await connectOttoman({
    connectionString: process.env.COUCHBASE_CONNECTION_STRING,
    bucketName: 'default',
    username: process.env.COUCHBASE_USERNAME,
    password: process.env.COUCHBASE_PASSWORD,
  });
  await startOttoman();

  clusterInstance = await couchbase.connect(
    process.env.COUCHBASE_CONNECTION_STRING,
    {
      username: process.env.COUCHBASE_USERNAME,
      password: process.env.COUCHBASE_PASSWORD,
      configProfile: 'wanDevelopment',
    }
  );
};

connectToCouchbase().catch(console.error);

export const getCluster = () => {
  if (!clusterInstance) {
    throw new Error('Couchbase cluster not initialized');
  }
  return clusterInstance;
};

export * from 'ottoman';
```

Once connected, Ottoman provides the interface for defining models and interacting with them. At the same time, we also initialize and store a separate clusterInstance using the Couchbase Node.js SDK. This gives us low-level access to Couchbase features beyond what Ottoman provides, for example, if we later need to work directly with key-value operations, indexes, or run raw data queries.

The module exports everything from Ottoman, so we can use those APIs throughout the app, and also provides a getCluster() function for retrieving the Couchbase cluster instance once it's connected. This gives us flexibility: we can build most of our app using Ottoman but still drop down to the raw Couchbase SDK whenever we need full control.

Now that we've configured the data layer, our back end is ready to store and retrieve vector data alongside standard document data like articles and users.

Key Takeaways

In this chapter, we focused on structuring the back end to support vector search functionality. We introduced a dedicated services folder to house vector-related logic, carefully modeled the article entity as the primary object for embeddings, and established a flexible and maintainable connection to the Couchbase database. This foundation ensures that our application is well prepared to generate and store vector embeddings in the chapters ahead.

Key takeaways from this chapter include the following:

- We introduced a services/ folder to house embedding and search logic, keeping it cleanly separated from the rest of the application architecture.

- We designed the Article model to include a new embedding field, setting the stage for incorporating vector search.

- We briefly reviewed the User, Comment, and Tag models, highlighting how they relate to articles.

- We configured a shared database connection using both Ottoman.js and the Couchbase Node.js SDK, giving us flexibility to work at both the model and raw query levels.

With the back-end structure, database connection, and core model in place, we're now ready to build the vector embedding generation service that will bring search relevance to life.

CHAPTER 6

Building the Vector Embedding Generation Service

In the last chapter, we laid the foundation for vector search by structuring the back end and defining the core data models. It's time to bring that structure to life with functionality that can generate vector embeddings from article content.

This chapter will walk you through building a service that transforms plain text into high-dimensional vectors that make vector search possible.

Structuring the Embedding Service

The vector embedding generation service will generate embeddings for articles and store them in the database. This service will be a critical component of the blog platform, as it will be the foundation for enabling users to search for articles based on semantic similarity and relevance.

The services/ folder at the project's root will contain all the vector embedding creation and search functionality. The contents of this folder are where we'll define the logic for generating embeddings, storing them in the database, and performing similarity searches. Let's start by first properly structuring the services/ folder to maintain separation of concerns and keep the code organized.

When we think about the operations of the vector search service in the application, we can break it down into its distinct components.

- New article or edit an existing article:
  - Generate a vector embedding for the article.
  - Save the vector embedding to the database.

- User search query:
  - Generate a vector embedding for the search query.
  - Perform a similarity search in the database.

We also introduce a couple of utilities to help us with vector operations; namely, we'll wish to help with the following:

- Validating text input for generating embeddings.
- Handling errors that may occur during the vector operations.

Lastly, we'll need a client to interact with the OpenAI API to generate embeddings. You started creating a services/ folder earlier, but now, let's put it all together. With these components in mind, let's structure the services/ folder as follows:

```
services/
├── clients/
│       ├── couchbaseClient.js
│       ├── openaiClient.js
├── embeddings/
│       ├── createEmbedding.js
│       ├── saveEmbedding.js
├── search/
│       ├── embedQuery.js
│       ├── performSearch.js
├── utils/
│       ├── errorHandlers.js
│       ├── validateText.js
```

It may be helpful to see the flow of interactions between these components for the two most common use cases, which are creating embeddings for articles and performing searches based on user queries. Let's visualize the flow for these operations as shown in the diagram on page 49.

The flow for a new article begins when the application passes the article content to validateText.js to ensure it meets quality standards before proceeding. If the input passes validation, createEmbedding.js invokes the OpenAI client via openaiClient.js to generate a vector embedding. The resulting embedding is then stored using saveEmbedding.js, which handles the database operations. Throughout this process, errorHandlers.js ensures any issues are handled gracefully.

The user query flow starts when the application receives a search query and passes it to embedQuery.js to generate a vector embedding for the search text. The code then uses the OpenAI client to create this query embedding. It passes the embedding to performSearch.js, which runs a similarity search against the stored article embeddings to find relevant results. Like the article flow, the

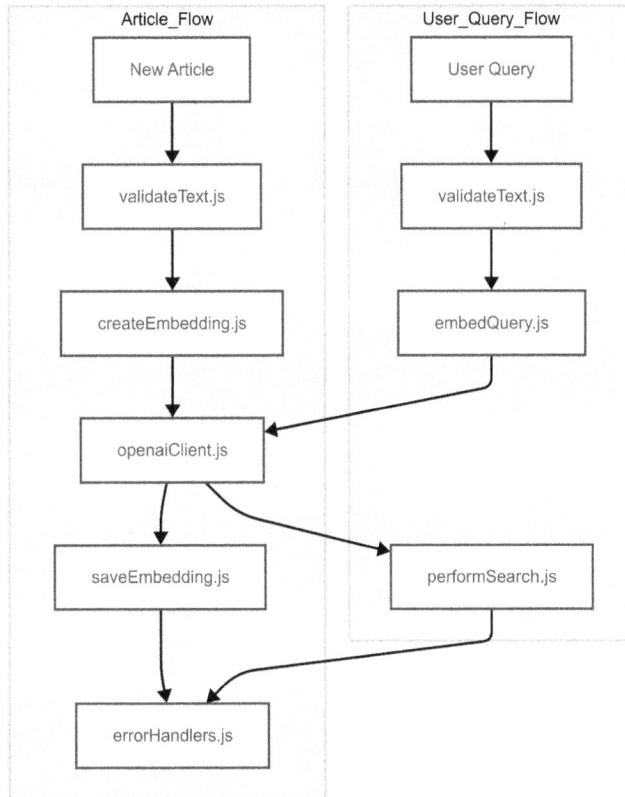

process includes validation and error handling to ensure smooth operation and accurate search results.

Building the Utilities

Before we dive into the core functionality of the vector embedding generation service, we'll start by building the utilities that handle text validation and error management. These tools ensure the system performs vector operations correctly and responds gracefully to errors.

The services/utils/ folder at the project's root will contain the utilities. This folder will include the logic for validating text input and handling errors. Let's start by creating the services/utils/ folder and structuring it as follows:

```
utils/
├── validateText.js
├── errorHandlers.js
```

Next, we create the validateText.js functionality.

Validating Text Input

The validateText.js utility will validate text input before generating vector embeddings. This utility ensures that the text input meets the requirements for generating embeddings and appropriately handles errors.

You might wonder why validating text input matters before generating embeddings. Besides general data quality and security concerns, generating vector embeddings involves real computational and financial costs. Validation ensures we generate embeddings only for meaningful, expected input.

Here's an example of what the validateText.js utility might look like. The actual validations you'll want in your application may vary, depending on your requirements, but this example should give you a good starting point:

```
implementing_vector_generation_service/validateText.js
import { ValidationError } from './errorHandlers';

const validateText = (text) => {
  if (typeof text !== 'string') {
    throw new ValidationError(
      'Input must be a string'
    );
  }

  if (text.trim() === '') {
    throw new ValidationError(
      'Input cannot be empty or just whitespace'
    );
  }

  const maxLength = 5000; // Adjust as necessary
  if (text.length > maxLength) {
    throw new ValidationError(
      `Input text exceeds maximum length of ${maxLength} characters`
    );
  }

  // Define a minimum length for the text
  const minLength = 5; // Adjust as necessary
  if (text.length < minLength) {
    throw new ValidationError(
      `Input text is too short, must be at least ${minLength} characters`
    );
  }

  // Check for repetitive content (such as too many duplicate words)
  const words = text.split(' ');
  const uniqueWords = new Set(words);
  // More than 70% repetitive words
  if (uniqueWords.size / words.length < 0.3) {
    throw new ValidationError(
```

```
      'Input text is too repetitive'
    );
  }

  // Check for excessive punctuation
  const excessivePunctuationRegex = /[!?.]{5,}/;
  if (excessivePunctuationRegex.test(text)) {
    throw new ValidationError(
      'Input text contains excessive punctuation'
    );
  }

  return true;
};

export default validateText;
```

In the preceding code, we're defining a validateText function that takes a text input as a parameter and performs various validations on the input. The function checks if the input is a string, is not empty or just whitespace, does not exceed a maximum length, meets a minimum length, is not too repetitive, and does not contain excessive punctuation. If any validations fail, the function throws a ValidationError with an appropriate error message. If all validations pass, the function returns true.

You may have noticed that the preceding code uses ValidationError, which imports from the errorHandlers.js utility. However, the utility doesn't exist yet, so let's create it next.

Handling Errors

The errorHandlers.js utility handles errors during vector embedding operations. It defines custom error classes the application can use to throw and catch specific errors. These classes provide more context and detail, making debugging and resolving issues easier.

Here's an example of what the errorHandlers.js utility might look like. The actual error classes you define may vary, depending on your requirements, but, as previously, this example should give you a good starting point:

```
implementing_vector_generation_service/errorHandlers.js
class ValidationError extends Error {
  constructor(message) {
    super(message);
    this.name = 'ValidationError';
    Error.captureStackTrace(this, this.constructor);
  }
}
```

At this point in our application development, we only create a single custom error class, ValidationError, which extends the built-in Error class. The ValidationError class takes a message parameter and sets the error name to ValidationError. We also use Error.captureStackTrace to capture the stack trace of the error, which can be helpful for debugging purposes. The ValidationError class throws validation errors when text input doesn't meet the requirements for generating vector embeddings.

As we build out further our application in the following chapters, we'll define additional custom error classes to handle different types of errors that may occur during the vector embedding operations. The ValidationError class will be a foundation for our error-handling strategy.

With the utilities for text validation and error handling in place, we've created a foundation that makes our vector embedding service easier to refactor and maintain. These utilities ensure valid text input and proper error handling during vector operations. Next, we'll implement the logic to persist embeddings, beginning with creating saveEmbedding.js in the services/embeddings/ folder.

Storing Embeddings in the Database

The saveEmbedding.js module stores embeddings in the database alongside their corresponding articles. Storing this data together enables efficient similarity searches based on vector distance.

We'll place the saveEmbedding.js file inside the services/embeddings/ folder at the root of our project. Let's create this folder and structure it as follows if you haven't already:

```
embeddings/
├── createEmbedding.js
├── saveEmbedding.js
```

In this section, we'll only focus on the saveEmbedding.js functionality, but you can see that we also have created a createEmbedding.js file. We'll build out the functionality of generating article embeddings in Creating Vector Embeddings, on page 55. For now, let's focus on storing the embeddings in the database.

The core responsibility of saveEmbedding.js is to store the embedding and its related article in the database. Since we're using Couchbase for this project, the save function will utilize Couchbase's document database capabilities. Here's an outline of the steps we'll take:

1. *Establish a database connection*: Connect to the Couchbase instance using the credentials from the configuration.

2. *Prepare the embedding data*: Ensure the embedding and associated article data are ready to be stored in a document.

3. *Insert the embedding into the database*: Insert the article and its embedding into Couchbase in a specific bucket.

The following diagram shows the step-by-step flow between the components, saving the embedding for the database.

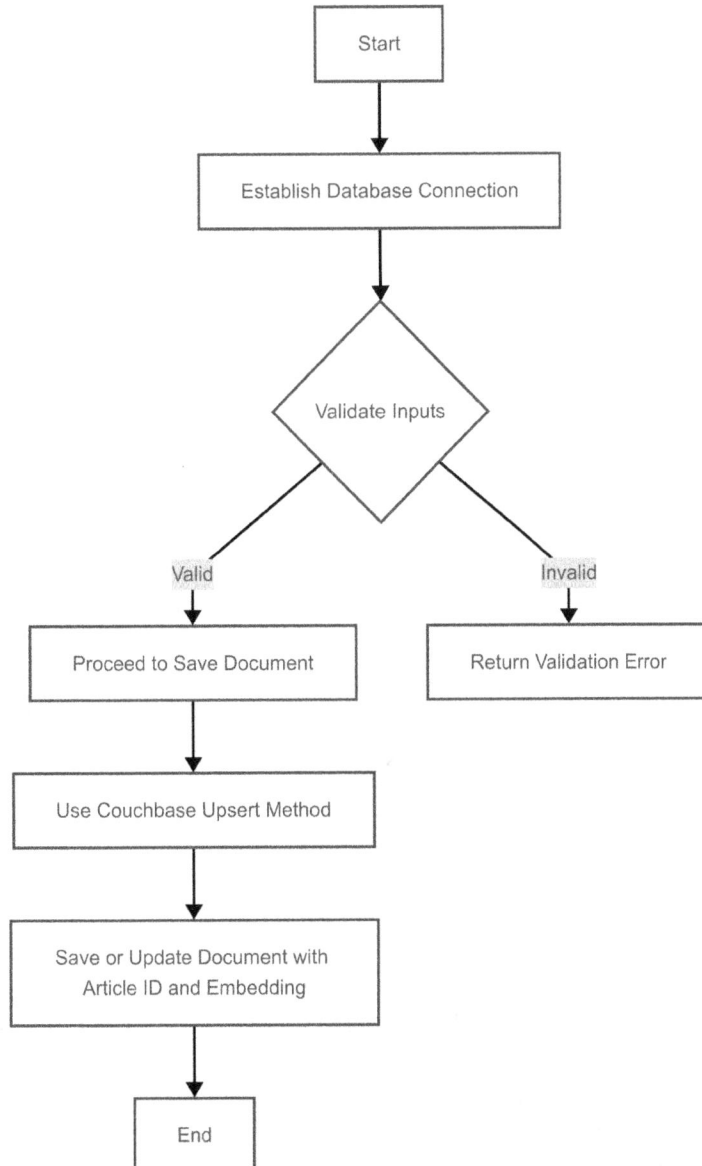

```
                    ┌─────────────┐
                    │    Start    │
                    └─────────────┘
                           │
                           ▼
            ┌──────────────────────────────┐
            │ Establish Database Connection │
            └──────────────────────────────┘
                           │
                           ▼
                        ◇ Validate Inputs ◇
                    ┌──────┴───────────┐
                  Valid              Invalid
                    │                   │
                    ▼                   ▼
        ┌─────────────────────┐  ┌──────────────────────┐
        │ Proceed to Save     │  │ Return Validation     │
        │ Document            │  │ Error                 │
        └─────────────────────┘  └──────────────────────┘
                    │
                    ▼
        ┌─────────────────────────┐
        │ Use Couchbase Upsert    │
        │ Method                  │
        └─────────────────────────┘
                    │
                    ▼
        ┌─────────────────────────┐
        │ Save or Update Document │
        │ with Article ID and     │
        │ Embedding               │
        └─────────────────────────┘
                    │
                    ▼
            ┌─────────────┐
            │     End     │
            └─────────────┘
```

Now, let's walk through an implementation of this in the saveEmbedding.js file:

```
implementing_vector_generation_service/saveEmbedding.js
import Article from '../models/Article';
import { ValidationError } from '../utils/errorHandlers';

// Function to save embedding and article data
const saveEmbedding = async (articleId, articleContent, embedding) => {
  if (!articleId || !embedding || !articleContent) {
    throw new ValidationError(
      'Article ID, content, and embedding are required to save.'
    );
  }

  try {
    // Find the existing article or create a new instance
    let article = await Article.findById(articleId);

    if (!article) {
      article = new Article({
        slug: articleContent.slug,  // Article slug
        title: articleContent.title,  // Article title
        description: articleContent.description,  // Article description
        body: articleContent.body,  // Article content
        author: articleContent.author,  // Article author ID
        tagList: articleContent.tagList,  // Tags associated with the article
        favoritesCount: 0,  // Initialize favorites count
        comments: [],  // Initialize comments
        embedding  // Save the embedding
      });
    } else {
      // Update the existing article's embedding
      article.embedding = embedding;
    }

    // Save the article with its embedding
    await article.save();
    console.log('Article and embedding saved successfully');
  } catch (error) {
    console.error('Error saving article and embedding:', error);
    throw error;
  }
};

export default saveEmbedding;
```

In the preceding code, we're defining a saveEmbedding function that takes an articleId, articleContent, and embedding as parameters. The function first checks if the required parameters are provided and throws a ValidationError if any are missing. It then attempts to find the existing article in the database based on the articleId. If the article does not exist, the code creates a new instance of the Article model with the article data and the embedding. If the article exists, the embedding is updated. Finally, the article with its embedding is saved to the database using the save method.

Updating an article's embedding is essential because its usefulness depends on how well it reflects the underlying content. If the article changes, its embedding should be updated, too, ensuring that search results remain accurate and relevant. Later, we'll explore optimizing this process by detecting meaningful changes before triggering updates. We've successfully defined the logic for saving embeddings to the database for now. Let's move on to generating embeddings for articles in the next section.

Creating Vector Embeddings

The createEmbedding.js file generates vector embeddings for articles based on their content. These embeddings capture the semantic meaning and context of each article, enabling similarity searches that return relevant results. To write code that is reusable, we'll also use this service to generate embeddings for user search queries.

Ready to begin writing the creation service? Let's get into it!

Designing the Create Embedding Logic

The core responsibility of createEmbedding.js is to generate a vector embedding for the article content. Since we're using the OpenAI API for this project, the create function will utilize the API to generate the embeddings. Here's an outline of the steps we'll take:

1. *Connect to the OpenAI API*: Use the OpenAI client to establish a connection to the OpenAI API.

2. *Prepare the article content*: Ensure the article content is ready to be passed to the API for embedding generation.

3. *Generate the embedding*: Use the OpenAI API to generate the vector embedding for the article content.

4. *Store the embedding*: Save the generated embedding in the database using the saveEmbedding.js functionality.

The flow of interactions for generating an embedding involves several key components:

- User submits a new article to the back-end API.
- Back-end API triggers the createEmbedding.js function.
- createEmbedding.js sends article content to the OpenAI API.

- OpenAI API returns the generated embedding.
- createEmbedding.js calls saveEmbedding.js with the embedding.
- saveEmbedding.js saves the embedding to the Couchbase database.
- Couchbase database confirms the save to saveEmbedding.js.
- saveEmbedding.js acknowledges the save to createEmbedding.js.
- createEmbedding.js notifies the back-end API of success.
- Back-end API confirms article saved with embedding to the User.

This sequence ensures the article content is processed into an embedding and reliably stored in the database before confirming success to the user.

Before we begin writing the code for the createEmbedding.js functionality, we must first create the OpenAI client functionality that will allow us to connect to the OpenAI API. With a good sense of how the creation of embeddings will flow in the service, let's take a moment to build the OpenAI client in the services /clients/ folder.

Designing the OpenAI API Client

The OpenAI client will connect to the OpenAI API and generate vector embeddings for text input. This client will provide an interface for interacting with the API and handling its responses. By encapsulating the functionality of connecting to the OpenAI API in a client, we can easily reuse the client across different application parts and maintain a consistent way of interacting with the API.

The OpenAI client will live in the services/clients/ folder at the project's root. The folder contains the logic for connecting to the OpenAI API and generating vector embeddings. Let's start by creating the services/clients/ folder and structuring it as follows if you haven't already:

```
clients/
├── openaiClient.js
```

This section will focus on implementing the openaiClient.js module, which handles the connection to the OpenAI API and the generation of vector embeddings.

The core responsibility of the OpenAI client is to connect to the OpenAI API and generate vector embeddings for text input. The client will provide an interface for interacting with the OpenAI API and handling the responses from the API. Here's an outline of the steps we'll take:

1. *Connect to the OpenAI API*: Establish a connection to the OpenAI API using the API key.

2. *Generate the embedding*: Use the OpenAI API to generate the vector embedding for the text input.

3. *Handle the response*: Parse and process the response from the OpenAI API to extract the embedding.

With the steps we need to accomplish in mind, let's walk through an implementation of this in the openaiClient.js file. We're building using the OpenAI Embeddings API documentation[1] as a reference.

Here's an example of what the openaiClient.js functionality might look like:

```
implementing_vector_generation_service/openaiClient.js
import OpenAI from 'openai';
// Importing custom error class for API errors
import { EmbeddingServiceError, ValidationError } from '../utils/errorHandlers';
// Importing validateText utility for input validation
import validateText from '../utils/validateText';

const OPENAI_API_KEY = process.env.OPENAI_API_KEY;

// Creating an instance with the provided configuration
const client = new OpenAI({
  apiKey: OPENAI_API_KEY,
});

// Function to generate embedding for a given text
const callEmbeddingAPI = async (text) => {
  try {
    validateText(text);

    // Making a request to OpenAI Embeddings API
    const response = await client.embeddings.create({
      // Use appropriate model for generating embeddings
      model: 'text-embedding-ada-002',
      input: text,
    });

    // Extract the embedding from the response
    const embedding = response.data[0]?.embedding;
    if (!embedding) {
      throw new EmbeddingServiceError(
        'Failed to retrieve embedding from response.'
      );
    }

    return embedding;
```

```
  } catch (error) {
    if (error instanceof OpenAI.APIError) {
      console.error(
        `OpenAI API Error [${error.status}]: ${error.message}`
      );
    } else if (error instanceof ValidationError) {
      console.error(
        `Validation Error: ${error.message}`
      );
    } else if (error instanceof EmbeddingServiceError) {
      console.error(
        `Embedding Service Error: ${error.message}`
      );
    } else {
      console.error(
        'Unexpected Error:', error
      );
    }
    throw error;
  }
};

export { callEmbeddingAPI };
```

We should highlight several key components of this code. First, we're using the OpenAI Node.js SDK[2] to build the client. This SDK provides a convenient way to interact with the OpenAI API for embeddings and other services.

We're also using the validateText utility we built earlier to ensure the text input is valid before sending it to the API for embedding generation. This is a good practice to ensure the input is clean and meaningful before proceeding with the embedding generation process.

The way we're handling errors is also meaningful. We're catching different types of errors, such as API, validation, and unexpected errors, and logging them appropriately. This helps us identify and resolve issues quickly and efficiently. *However, did you notice something amiss about our error handling?* We're using a custom EmbeddingServiceError class that we've not defined yet!

Let's reopen the errorHandlers.js file in the services/utils/ folder and add the Embedding ServiceError class to it right now.

```
implementing_vector_generation_service/errorHandlers.js
class EmbeddingServiceError extends Error {
  constructor(message, status) {
    super(message);
    this.name = 'EmbeddingServiceError';
```

---

2.   https://github.com/openai/openai-node

```
    this.status = status;
    Error.captureStackTrace(this, this.constructor);
  }
}
```

The preceding code defines an EmbeddingServiceError class that extends the built-in Error class. The EmbeddingServiceError class takes a message and status parameter and sets the error name to EmbeddingServiceError. We also use Error.captureStackTrace to capture the stack trace of the error, which can be helpful for debugging purposes. The EmbeddingServiceError class will handle the mistakes during interactions with the OpenAI API. With the EmbeddingServiceError class defined, we've successfully built the OpenAI client that will allow us to connect to the OpenAI API and generate vector embeddings for text input. This client will be a critical component of the vector embedding service, as it will enable us to create embeddings for articles and user search queries.

With the OpenAI client built, we're ready to write the code for the createEmbedding.js functionality. Let's move on to creating the functionality for generating embeddings for articles.

Writing the Create Embedding Logic

The createEmbedding.js will use the earlier code we built to abstract the OpenAI API client, text validation, and error handling. As a result of our earlier work, the code for generating embeddings for articles and search queries will be concise and focused on the core functionality of generating embeddings. Let's dive into the code for the createEmbedding.js functionality.

Implementing_vector_generation_service/createEmbedding.js

```javascript
// Importing the OpenAI client for generating embeddings
import { callEmbeddingAPI } from '../clients/openaiClient';
// Importing validateText utility for input validation
import validateText from '../utils/validateText';
// Importing saveEmbedding to store the generated embedding
import { saveEmbedding } from './saveEmbedding';

/**
 * Create an embedding for the given content and
 * either save it or return it based on the type.
 *
 * @param {string} identifier - A unique identifier for the
 * entity (for instance article ID, query ID).
 * @param {string} content - The content for which the embedding
 * is to be created (for instance article body, user query).
 * @param {string} type - The type of content (such as 'article').
 * @returns {Promise<object | void>} - Returns the embedding if
 * the type is 'query', otherwise saves it.
 */
```

```javascript
const createEmbedding = async (identifier, content, type) => {
  try {
    validateText(content);
    const embedding = await callEmbeddingAPI(content);
    if (type === 'article') {
      await saveEmbedding(identifier, embedding, type);
      console.log(
        `Successfully saved embedding for article ID: ${identifier}`
      );
    } else if (type === 'query') {
      console.log(
        `Generated embedding for query with ID: ${identifier}`
      );
      return embedding;
    }
  } catch (error) {
    console.error(
      'Error creating embedding:', error.message
    );
    throw error;
  }
};

export { createEmbedding };
```

In the preceding code, we're defining a createEmbedding function that takes an identifier, content, and type as parameters. The function first validates the content using the validateText utility to ensure the input is valid. It then generates an embedding for the content using the callEmbeddingAPI function from the OpenAI client. Finally, it saves the embedding in the database using the saveEmbedding function if the embedding is for an article. Otherwise, it returns the embedding for a search query. The function logs a success message when it successfully creates and saves or returns the embedding. It also logs an error message when an error occurs during the process.

This code is versatile and flexible in that it can generate embeddings for different types of content in the application, whether an article or a user search query. By writing the function in a generic, reusable way, we ensure consistency across the application and simplify future maintenance. With the core embedding generation logic in place, our vector generation service is complete and ready to power vector search.

Key Takeaways

In this chapter, we built our application's core functionality required for generating vector embeddings. By layering together reusable utilities, a modular OpenAI client, and structured service logic, we laid the technical foundation that powers our search experience.

These are the key points to take with you into the next chapters:

- We introduced a clear service structure for the vector embedding functionality, separating concerns across embeddings/, clients/, search/, and utils/ folders.

- Utilities such as validateText.js and errorHandlers.js ensure the system processes only clean, meaningful input and gracefully handles failures.

- The saveEmbedding.js module handles the persistence of embeddings into the database, ensuring that updated content results in updated embeddings.

- The openaiClient.js file wraps the logic for interacting with the OpenAI API, including validation and error management.

- The createEmbedding.js function ties everything together, offering a reusable way to generate embeddings for articles and user queries.

With our vector embedding service fully operational, we can use these embeddings to implement similarity search across article content in the next chapter.

CHAPTER 7

Creating a Vector Search Service

You have reached an exciting milestone in your journey to master vector search! In the previous chapter, we laid the groundwork by building the core functionality to generate and store vector embeddings. It's time to take the next significant step: creating a vector search service that leverages those embeddings to find relevant content.

Imagine providing users with search results that genuinely understand the context and meaning behind their queries rather than just matching keywords. This is the power of vector search, and in this chapter we'll transform our embeddings into a practical and useful search experience. We'll continue to do so by building further our fully featured Node.js back-end blog platform. As we progress, remember that at the end of this book you'll have a completed application; the techniques, concepts, and skills you learn can be applied to various projects and domains.

Without further ado, let's get going!

Generating Embeddings for User Queries

In the search service layer, the user query journey begins when the user enters a search term. Once the query is received, the service converts it into a vector representation using an embedding model. This transformation is crucial because it allows the system to compare the meaning behind the query with stored data. The query vector is then compared against the embeddings of articles in the database, using the dot product as the similarity metric.

The system then ranks the results based on the similarity scores generated by the comparison. Higher similarity scores indicate closer matches between the user's search term and the stored data. The system can return the top results to the user depending on how we set up the ranking algorithm. The system repeats this process whenever the user enters a new search query, ensuring the search results remain relevant and up-to-date.

The first step in the search process is to convert the user query into a vector embedding. The good news is that you've already become well-versed in this process! We have also set up the necessary skeleton for the search service in the services/ folder by scaffolding the file structure and defining the core functions.

We'll use the functionality in embeddings/createEmbedding.js to generate the vector representation of the user query. search/embedQuery.js will call this function and handle the flow to the next step in the search process. We can reuse the existing embedding generation logic because we built createEmbedding to be versatile and flexible, as the process of generating an embedding is essentially the same regardless of the input source. The primary difference is what the final output of the createEmbedding function is, and we can see that in the following code snippet from that function:

implementing_vector_generation_service/createEmbedding.js
```
if (type === 'article') {
  await saveEmbedding(identifier, embedding, type);
  console.log(
    `Successfully saved embedding for article ID: ${identifier}`
  );
} else if (type === 'query') {
  console.log(
    `Generated embedding for query with ID: ${identifier}`
  );
  return embedding;
}
```

This snippet shows that the function can differentiate between an article and a query based on the type parameter. For an article, the system saves the embedding to the database using saveEmbedding, while it returns the embedding to the caller for a query. This flexibility allows us to seamlessly integrate the embedding generation process into the search service without duplicating code or creating unnecessary complexity.

If you're eager to test how query embeddings are generated before wiring them into the full search flow, you can run a quick CLI utility we've prepared for that purpose. Before running it, make sure you've set your OpenAI API key in a .env file at the root of the project or in your shell environment using the variable OPENAI_API_KEY.

creating_vector_search_service/testEmbeddingCLI.js
```
import 'dotenv/config';
import readline from 'readline';
```

```
import { createEmbedding } from '../embeddings/createEmbedding.js';
import { ValidationError } from '../utils/errorHandlers.js';

const rl = readline.createInterface({
  input: process.stdin,
  output: process.stdout,
});

rl.question('Enter a search query: ', async (query) => {
  try {
    if (!query) {
      throw new ValidationError('Query content is missing', 'query');
    }

    const embedding = await createEmbedding('cli-test-query', query, 'query');
    console.log('\nFirst 5 dimensions of the embedding:\n');
    console.log(embedding.slice(0, 5).map(n => n.toFixed(4)).join(', ') + '...');
  } catch (error) {
    console.error('Error generating embedding:', error.message);
  } finally {
    rl.close();
  }
});
```

To run the CLI utility, execute the following command in your terminal:

bash node testEmbeddingCLI.js

Enter a search query when prompted. The script generates an embedding using the OpenAI API and prints the first few dimensions of the resulting vector. This gives you a quick, firsthand look at what embedding a query looks like before you integrate it into the broader search system.

After generating a query embedding from the command line, you can now integrate that functionality into the service layer. Build out the code in embedQuery.js to move one step closer to a fully functional vector search service.

```
creating_vector_search_service/embedQuery.js
import { createEmbedding } from '../embeddings/createEmbedding';
import { performSearch } from './performSearch';
import { ValidationError } from '../utils/errorHandlers';

/**
 * Embeds a user query and performs a search.
 *
 * @param {string} queryId - The unique ID for the query.
 * @param {string} query - The search query entered by the user.
 * @returns {Promise<object>} - The search results.
 */
```

```javascript
const embedAndSearch = async (queryId, query) => {
  try {
    if (!query) {
      throw new ValidationError('Query content is missing', 'query');
    }

    const queryEmbedding = await createEmbedding(
      queryId, query, 'query'
    );
    const searchResults = await performSearch(queryEmbedding);

    return searchResults;
  } catch (error) {
    if (error instanceof ValidationError) {
      console.error(
        `Validation Error: ${error.message}, Field: ${error.field}`
      );
    } else {
      console.error(
        `Error: ${error.message}`
      );
    }
    throw error;
  }
};

export { embedAndSearch };
```

The embedAndSearch function is the entry point for embedding a user query and performing the vector search. First, it validates the query content to ensure it's not empty. If it passes validation, it calls createEmbedding to generate the query embedding and then passes the new embedding to performSearch to find the most relevant articles. If an error occurs during the process, the system catches and handles it appropriately to remain robust and user-friendly.

Speaking about validation, you may have noticed we included a ValidationError class in the error handling, but we have not yet written the code for it. This will be a new custom error class similar to the others we have defined, like EmbeddingServiceError. Let's implement that now by reopening the errorHandlers.js file in utils/ and adding the following code after the existing error classes:

creating_vector_search_service/errorHandlers.js

```javascript
class ValidationError extends Error {
    constructor(message) {
        super(message);
        this.name = 'ValidationError';
        Error.captureStackTrace(this, this.constructor);
    }
}
```

Make sure to add the new ValidationError to the export statement at the end of the file to make it accessible to other application parts like embedQuery.js. With this new error class in place, we can now handle validation errors in a more structured and consistent manner, improving the overall reliability of our system.

The code for embedQuery is lightweight because it leverages the composability of the existing services and functions we've built and will continue to build out. While vector search is a complex topic, implementing it in our codebases doesn't have to be equally complex.

Before we build out the logic for performing similarity searches using the dot product, let's quickly recap the flow of the user query embedding and search process from the perspective of the invoked functions.

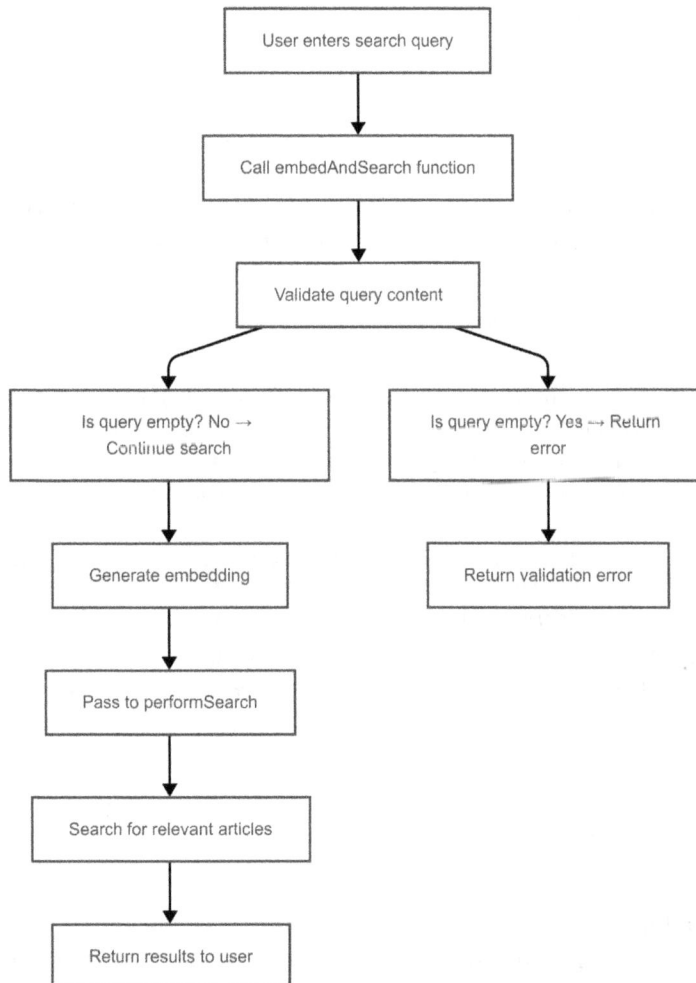

- The user enters a search query, and the system calls the embedAndSearch function.

- The query content is validated to ensure it's not empty.

- The query is converted into a vector embedding using the createEmbedding function.

- The query embedding is passed to the performSearch function to find the most relevant articles.

- The search results are returned to the user, completing the search process.

As you can see, we're close to having a fully functional vector search service. The next step is to implement the similarity search logic at the heart of a vector search service.

Performing Similarity Searches

In this section, we'll tackle building the search functionality, specifically focusing on calculating the similarity between a user query and stored article embeddings, using the dot product. We'll walk through the process of building out the performSearch.js file, and to better understand the dot product, we'll even calculate it manually.

Quick Refresher: Why Use Cosine Similarity and Dot Product?

Cosine similarity and dot product measure the semantic alignment between vectors. Cosine similarity calculates how closely two vectors point in the same direction, disregarding their magnitude. Dot product also focuses on direction, highlighting semantic alignment. Both metrics help surface content conceptually related, not just syntactically matched, to user queries.

We now have embeddings for both the search query and the articles. The embeddings, however, are just the starting point! Our task is to compare the query vector embedding against the stored article embeddings and determine how similar they are. When the vectors are closer, the articles align more closely with the user's query, have higher relevance, and deserve a higher rank in the search results. The dot product plays a key role in this comparison, though you could also use other similarity metrics, such as cosine similarity or Euclidean distance.

The formula for the dot product involves multiplying corresponding elements from the two vectors and summing the results. To help understand the concept, let's examine a simple version of the dot product calculation with two small vectors.

Perhaps you have two vectors, A and B, represented like so:

```
A = [1, 2, 3]
B = [4, 5, 6]
```

Each vector has three elements, which means they are three-dimensional vectors. To calculate the dot product, we multiply the corresponding elements of the two vectors and sum the results:

```
(1 * 4) + (2 * 5) + (3 * 6) = 4 + 10 + 18 = 32
```

The dot product of A and B is 32. This value tells us how closely the vectors A and B are aligned in vector space. The higher the dot product, the more similar the vectors are in direction and the more related the content they represent.

What about the case where the vectors are orthogonal or perpendicular to each other? In that case, the dot product will be zero, indicating that the vectors are not aligned. Understanding orthogonality is crucial as we build our search system. Let's see an example with two orthogonal vectors:

```
C = [1, 0, 0]
D = [0, 1, 0]
```

Here's the dot product of C and D:

```
(1 * 0) + (0 * 1) + (0 * 0) = 0 + 0 + 0 = 0
```

A result of 0 indicates the vectors C and D are orthogonal, or perpendicular, to each other. Orthogonality is a fundamental concept in vector mathematics and enables us to measure the similarity between vectors in our search system.

In the context of our search service, each element in the vectors represents a specific feature that the embedding model has identified in the content. We can determine how closely the content aligns in vector space by multiplying corresponding features and summing the results.

Now that you have a solid understanding of the dot product and how it helps us measure similarity between vectors, let's build the logic for performing similarity searches in our search service. If you haven't already, start by creating the performSearch.js file in the services/search/ directory and implementing the core functionality for comparing query embeddings with stored article embeddings.

creating_vector_search_service/performSearch.js

```javascript
import { getAllStoredEmbeddings } from './fetchEmbeddings';
import { dotProduct } from '../utils/mathUtils';

/**
 * Perform similarity search by comparing query
 * embedding with stored embeddings.
 *
 * @param {Array} queryEmbedding - The query vector embedding.
 * @returns {Promise<Array>} - A ranked list of relevant articles
 * based on similarity.
 */
const performSearch = async (queryEmbedding) => {
  try {
    // Fetch all stored embeddings from Couchbase
    const storedEmbeddings = await getAllStoredEmbeddings();

    // Perform dot product for each article embedding
    const searchResults = storedEmbeddings.map(
      ({ articleId, embedding }) => {
      const similarityScore = dotProduct(queryEmbedding, embedding);
      return { articleId, similarityScore };
    });

    // Rank articles by similarity score in descending order
    searchResults.sort(
      (a, b) => b.similarityScore - a.similarityScore
    );

    return searchResults;  // Return ranked results
  } catch (error) {
    console.error(
      'Error performing similarity search:', error
    );
    throw error;
  }
};

export { performSearch };
```

In this implementation, we fetch the stored article embeddings from Couchbase using getAllStoredEmbeddings, which we need to implement next. Then we map over each article embedding and calculate the dot product with the query embedding. We store the article ID and the resulting similarity score, and finally, we sort the results by the similarity score in descending order so that the most relevant articles appear first.

The most helpful part of using the dot product is its simplicity and efficiency, especially when working with high-dimensional vectors or vectors with many elements. Unlike Euclidean distance, which focuses on the absolute difference between vectors, or cosine similarity, which measures the angles between vectors, the dot product homes in on the alignment of vectors. Its focus on alignment makes the dot product well suited for our search system. We want to know how much the user's query *aligns* with our stored articles, and the dot product allows us to capture this relationship.

Before we build the dot product calculation in the utils/ folder, let's ensure we have the functionality to retrieve the stored embeddings using Ottoman.js from Couchbase. Go ahead and create a new file called fetchEmbeddings.js in the services/search/ directory and add the following code:

creating_vector_search_service/fetchEmbeddings.js
```
import { getModel } from 'ottoman';

/**
 * Fetch all stored embeddings from Couchbase.
 *
 * @returns {Promise<Array>} - An array of objects containing
 * articleId and embeddings.
 */
const getAllStoredEmbeddings = async () => {
  try {
    const ArticleModel = getModel('Article');
    const articles = await ArticleModel.find(
      {}, { select: ['_id', 'embedding'] }
    );

    return articles.rows.map(article => ({
      articleId: article._id,
      embedding: article.embedding,
    }));
  } catch (error) {
    console.error(
      'Error fetching embeddings:', error.message
    );
    throw error;
  }
};

export { getAllStoredEmbeddings };
```

This function uses the Article model we defined earlier to fetch all articles from Couchbase and extract their IDs and embeddings. The resulting array of objects is what we need to perform the dot product calculation in the performSearch function. With this in place, we can build the dot product calculation in the mathUtils.js file in the utils/ directory.

```
creating_vector_search_service/mathUtils.js
import { VectorLengthError } from './errorHandlers';

/**
 * Calculate the dot product of two vectors.
 *
 * @param {Array} vectorA - The first vector.
 * @param {Array} vectorB - The second vector.
 * @returns {number} - The dot product of the two vectors.
 */
const dotProduct = (vectorA, vectorB) => {
  if (vectorA.length !== vectorB.length) {
    throw new VectorLengthError('Vectors must be of the same length');
  }

  return vectorA.reduce(
    (acc, curr, idx) => acc + curr * vectorB[idx], 0
  );
};

export { dotProduct };
```

The dotProduct function takes two vectors, checks that they have the same length, and then uses the reduce method to multiply corresponding elements and sum the results. The resulting value is the dot product of the two vectors, which helps us measure the similarity between the query embedding and the stored article embeddings. Like the previous code we implemented, we've also introduced a new custom error class, VectorLengthError, to handle cases where the vectors are not the same length. Once again, open the errorHandlers.js file in the utils\ directory, add the following code after the existing error classes, and make sure to add VectorLengthError to the export statement:

```
creating_vector_search_service/errorHandlers.js
class VectorLengthError extends Error {
    constructor(message) {
        super(message);
        this.name = 'VectorLengthError';
        Error.captureStackTrace(this, this.constructor);
    }
}
```

With both getAllStoredEmbeddings and dotProduct functions in place, the system is now ready to calculate the similarity between user queries and stored articles, using the dot product as the measure of relevance.

We've successfully implemented all the back-end functionality needed to perform vector search using the dot product as the similarity metric! It's a good moment to take a step back and appreciate your progress. You've built a robust system to generate embeddings for user queries and articles, compare them using the dot product, and return relevant search results.

Key Takeaways

In this chapter, you transformed the vector embeddings you've been generating into a working search feature. By building a modular service for embedding and comparing vectors, you took a significant step toward delivering meaningful, context-aware search results to users.

These are the key takeaways from this chapter:

- Using the dot product, you implemented a search service that embeds user queries and compares them to stored article embeddings.

- You reused your existing embedding logic by designing createEmbedding to support content and query inputs.

- You added input validation and introduced a ValidationError class to ensure reliable and secure search handling.

- You created a utility function to calculate the dot product and introduced a custom error for mismatched vector lengths.

Next, we'll focus on building a vector search index to optimize search performance and scalability.

CHAPTER 8

Creating a Vector Search Index

In Chapter 7, Creating a Vector Search Service, on page 63, we implemented vector search manually using dot product calculations, which gave us a solid grasp of the fundamentals. In this chapter, we'll take the next step by integrating Couchbase's native vector search indexing and using the Ottoman.js library to simplify query building. This approach will replace our manual vector operations, improving our application's performance, scalability, and maintainability.

Understanding Search Indexes

Before we build our vector search index, let's take a step back and understand what a search index is and why it's so important for optimizing search functionality.

A search index can be considered a database's roadmap for quickly finding data. Instead of scanning the entire dataset to find relevant information (which can be slow and inefficient, especially as the dataset grows), an index helps the database jump directly to the appropriate pieces of information. It acts like an efficient catalog or table of contents, making it easier for search engines or databases to retrieve results much faster.

For traditional databases, indexes are often built using keys or specific fields, like titles or tags, to make search queries more efficient. However, we're not just searching for exact matches in vector search. We're trying to find data conceptually or semantically similar to a given query. This is where a vector search index comes in.

Under the hood, vector search indexes use smart shortcuts to avoid comparing every single vector one by one. Instead of brute force, they use methods that group or organize vectors to speed up the search.

Some indexes use tree-like structures that split the data into smaller sections, so the search can focus only where it's most likely to find a match. Others use a method similar to hashing, where similar vectors are grouped into buckets. A third approach connects vectors into a kind of roadmap or graph, where the system can quickly move from one nearby vector to the next, getting closer to the best match step by step.

These techniques all aim to reduce the number of comparisons needed. The result is a faster and more scalable search. When you run a query, the index uses these shortcuts to quickly find a handful of promising candidates, then ranks them by similarity.

A vector search index optimizes searches that use vector embeddings. Instead of manually calculating this similarity between vectors (as we did in Chapter 7, Creating a Vector Search Service, on page 63), we can offload this task to a specialized database service, such as Couchbase, which can handle these operations much more efficiently.

Let's take a look at a diagram that illustrates the flow of a vector search index, as shown on page 77.

The key advantage of a search index is its speed. Instead of scanning through every piece of data in real time, the system compares the query vector against the pre-built indexed vectors in the search index. This comparison is where similarity metrics, such as the dot product or cosine similarity, come into play. These metrics measure how closely aligned the vectors are, which translates to how semantically similar the documents are to the query.

The system computes these similarity scores and ranks the documents by relevance. Documents with higher similarity scores appear at the top of the search results, ensuring that users receive the most relevant content first.

Now that we understand what a vector search index is and how it works, let's start building one using Couchbase and Ottoman.js.

Creating a Vector Search Index

Before continuing, make sure you've added at least a few articles to your blog platform and generated embeddings for them. If you haven't done this yet, you can either create original articles or use any existing content of yours. Follow the article spec[1] from the RealWorld project to ensure compatibility.

---

1.   https://realworld-docs.netlify.app/specifications/backend/endpoints/#create-article

```
┌─────────────────────────┐
│       User Query        │
└─────────────────────────┘
             │
             ▼
┌─────────────────────────┐
│  Transform to Embedding  │
└─────────────────────────┘
             │
             ▼
┌─────────────────────────┐
│      Query Vector        │
└─────────────────────────┘
             │
             ▼
┌─────────────────────────┐
│   Vector Search Index    │
└─────────────────────────┘
             │
             ▼
┌─────────────────────────┐
│ Compare with Indexed Vectors │
└─────────────────────────┘
             │
             ▼
┌─────────────────────────┐
│   Compute Similarity     │
└─────────────────────────┘
             │
             ▼
┌─────────────────────────┐
│    Rank by Relevance     │
└─────────────────────────┘
             │
             ▼
┌─────────────────────────┐
│    Return Top Results    │
└─────────────────────────┘
```

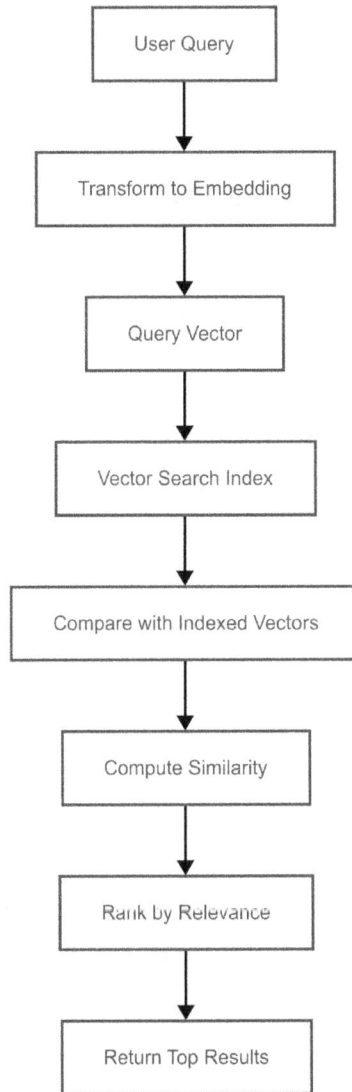

The vector search index will only work if vector embeddings are already saved in Couchbase—refer back to Chapter 7, Creating a Vector Search Service, on page 63, for details on how to do this.

This section will create a vector search index in Couchbase using the cbshell command-line interface. We'll set up the index to use the dot product as the similarity metric, allowing us to search for similar vectors in our database efficiently.

First of all, what is cbshell?[2] It's a command-line tool that allows you to interact with your database from the terminal. Other ways to work with your data include using a web interface or an IDE extension. However, when you're already in the terminal, using a CLI tool allows you to conveniently perform tasks without switching contexts.

Setting up cbshell is relatively straightforward. You need to provide it with configuration details pointing to your cluster and authentication information. Once you have that set up, you can run commands to interact with your database. In this case, the fastest way to get that configuration information is to log in to your Couchbase Capella account in a browser and follow a few steps. Let's make sure that's set up before we proceed.

Fetching Configuration Details for cbshell

To get your configuration details, navigate to your Couchbase Capella account[3] and follow these steps:

Click the Connect button from the dashboard view inside your cluster details. You'll see a page similar to this:

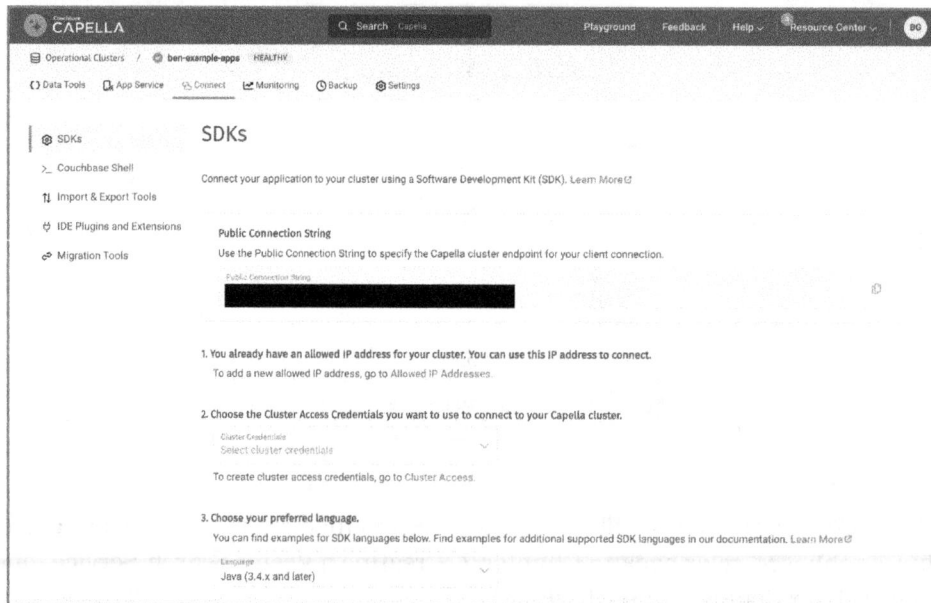

You'll notice a Couchbase Shell link on the left-hand navigation bar. That's where you should go next. Click that link.

---

2.   https://github.com/couchbaselabs/couchbase-shell
3.   https://cloud.couchbase.com

The CLI then presents options to configure your cbshell configuration file, such as which cluster credential to use. Once you've selected your desired credentials, copy the configuration details and paste them into a new file named config inside the .cbsh folder created after installing the CLI tool.

Finally, in the configuration file, replace the placeholder value for your password with your actual password.

Now that your setup is complete, you can use the cbshell CLI for all your database interactions.

Creating a Vector Search Index

Once we've created the new vector search index using cbshell, we can remove the manual dot product calculation from our codebase. Offloading the similarity calculations to the database will make our search operations more efficient and scalable.

You may be asking yourself why we didn't start with this approach. One of the best ways to learn how something works is to start from the first principles. By building the dot product calculation manually, you've hopefully gained a deeper understanding of how it all works under the hood. Now that we have that understanding, we can leverage Couchbase's built-in capabilities to handle this.

Let's go ahead and do it by first opening up the CLI:

```
./cbsh
```

You should see a prompt like this:

```
>
```

By invoking the buckets command, you can run a quick test command to see if everything is set up and working as expected. The buckets command will return the list of buckets in your cluster:

```
> buckets
```

If all is good, you'll see your buckets listed in an output similar to the one that follows. If not, or if you encounter any issues, you may need to revisit your configuration settings.

#	cluster	name	type	replicas	
0	default	beer-sample	couchbase	1	
1	default	default	couchbase	1	
2	default	targetBucket	couchbase	0	
3	default	travel-sample	couchbase	1	

We can create our vector search index now that we've confirmed that cbshell is working as expected. The command to create a new vector index is vector create-index. The command itself takes several arguments we will need to provide—namely, the name of the bucket where the embeddings are stored, the similarity metric to use, the name of the index we wish to create, the name of the field containing the embeddings, and the number of dimensions in the embeddings.

Since we're creating our application using dot product as the similarity metric, we'll use the following command to create the index:

```
creating_vector_search_index/cbshell_command_examples.sh
vector create-index \
    --bucket bucket_name \
    --similarity-metric dot_product
vector-search-index embedding 1536
```

In this command, replace name_of_your_bucket with the bucket's name where your embeddings are stored. The vector-search-index is the name of the index we're creating, embedding is the name of the field containing the embeddings, and 1536 is the number of dimensions in the embeddings. The number of dimensions should match the size of the embeddings you used when you created the embeddings for the documents in your database.

You can perform a quick check to ensure the index was created by querying for all the indexes, and you should see the new index in the list:

```
creating_vector_search_index/cbshell_command_examples.sh
query indexes
```

That's it! You've successfully created a vector search index in Couchbase using cbshell. This index will allow you to perform similarity searches more efficiently by offloading the heavy lifting of similarity calculations to the database. Let's integrate this index into our application using the Couchbase Node.js SDK and Ottoman.js. This part involves deleting code, which is always fun!

Integrating the Vector Search Index

We'll continue to use the Couchbase Node SDK and Ottoman.js to interact with the database and query the vector search index. By leveraging Ottoman.js, we can simplify the process of building and executing queries, making it easier to work with our vector search index.

The code we previously created in performSearch.js implements the similarity search logic. It currently uses the manual dot product calculation we built in utils/mathUtils.js to compare the query embedding with the embeddings stored in the database. We'll remove this manual calculation and replace it with a query to the vector search index we created in Couchbase.

We no longer need the utils/mathUtils.js file now that Couchbase handles vector similarity calculations for us. You can safely delete this file to clean up your codebase.

The new function will take the search query embedding from the user as an argument and return the most similar documents from the database based on the vector search index. Previously, performSearch operated in the following manner:

creating_vector_search_service/performSearch.js

```javascript
import { getAllStoredEmbeddings } from './fetchEmbeddings';
import { dotProduct } from '../utils/mathUtils';

/**
 * Perform similarity search by comparing query
 * embedding with stored embeddings.
 *
 * @param {Array} queryEmbedding - The query vector embedding.
 * @returns {Promise<Array>} - A ranked list of relevant articles
 * based on similarity.
 */
const performSearch = async (queryEmbedding) => {
  try {
    // Fetch all stored embeddings from Couchbase
    const storedEmbeddings = await getAllStoredEmbeddings();

    // Perform dot product for each article embedding
    const searchResults = storedEmbeddings.map(
      ({ articleId, embedding }) => {
      const similarityScore = dotProduct(queryEmbedding, embedding);
      return { articleId, similarityScore };
    });

    // Rank articles by similarity score in descending order
    searchResults.sort(
      (a, b) => b.similarityScore - a.similarityScore
    );

    return searchResults;  // Return ranked results
  } catch (error) {
    console.error(
      'Error performing similarity search:', error
    );
    throw error;
  }
};

export { performSearch };
```

The primary change we need to make is to introduce new functionality that only returns the articles most similar to the user query. Before, we needed to fetch all of the embeddings and calculate the dot product for each one. Now, we can query the vector search index in Couchbase to return only the most relevant documents. This shift provides a considerable performance improvement.

creating_vector_search_index/performSearch.js

```javascript
import { getCluster } from '../clients/couchbaseClient';
import couchbase from 'couchbase';

/**
 * Perform similarity search by comparing query embedding with
 * stored embeddings.
 *
 * @param {Array} queryEmbedding - The query vector embedding.
 * @returns {Promise<Array>} - A ranked list of relevant articles based
 * on similarity.
 */
const performSearch = async (queryEmbedding) => {
  try {
    const cluster = await getCluster();
    const scope = cluster.bucket('default').scope('_default');
    const searchIndex = 'vector-search-index';

    const searchReq = couchbase.SearchRequest.create(
      couchbase.VectorSearch.fromVectorQuery(
        couchbase.VectorQuery.create(
          "default.embedding", queryEmbedding
        ).numCandidates(5)
      )
    );

    const result = await scope.search(searchIndex, searchReq);

    return result.rows
      .map((row) => ({
        articleId: row.id.replace('embedding::', ''),
        similarityScore: row.score,
      }))
      .sort((a, b) => b.similarityScore - a.similarityScore);
  } catch (error) {
    console.error('Error performing similarity search:', error);
    throw error;
  }
};

export { performSearch };
```

In this implementation, we connect to the Couchbase cluster, access the target bucket and scope, and construct a vector search request using couchbase .VectorSearch.fromVectorQuery. This method takes the embedding field name and the query embedding as inputs. We specify how many top candidates to return (in this case, 5) and execute the query using scope.search. Results are mapped and ranked by similarity score before being returned to the user.

A single call to the vector search index now replaces the manual dot product logic we previously implemented. Here's a breakdown of the updated process:

- Initialize search by setting up a Couchbase cluster connection and accessing the target bucket and scope.

- Construct and send vector query using VectorQuery, then execute it on the "embeddings" field via the vector search index.

- Retrieve and map results from the top five matches based on similarity score, extracting articleId and similarityScore.

- Sort and return results in descending order by similarity before sending them back to the caller.

This streamlined flow shows how embedding-based search brings more meaning to user queries. Instead of relying on exact term matches, vector search enables semantic relevance by comparing embeddings across stored documents. The VectorQuery interface hides much of the operational complexity, letting developers focus on what they want to retrieve rather than how to retrieve it.

Scoping the search to a specific bucket and scope keeps the query efficient and ensures it operates only on the intended dataset. This design avoids unnecessary overhead and aligns well with how NoSQL JSON document databases organize data.

Because results include both content identifiers and similarity scores, they can be ranked and filtered based on relevance. This makes vector search a strong fit for use cases like personalized recommendations, semantic filtering, and natural language search all within a consistent and scalable interface.

Key Takeaways

This chapter shifted from manual similarity calculations to a more sustainable, performant, and advanced approach: creating a vector search index within a data platform like Couchbase. While the previous chapter introduced us to the fundamentals of vector search, this chapter took it further by leveraging a NoSQL database's capabilities to handle these operations efficiently. By offloading the search calculations to the database, we simplified our back end and optimized the search service's performance, transforming it into a scalable solution ready for production.

Here are the key takeaways:

- Setting up a vector search index reduces back-end complexity by managing similarity calculations at the database level.

- The integration with Couchbase allows us to handle large datasets seamlessly, making the service faster and more reliable.

- Leveraging Ottoman.js for query management keeps the codebase clean and modular, supporting future growth and scalability.

Looking ahead, we'll build on this foundation by integrating user-facing features into our back end, such as finishing the search API to make the vector search functionality accessible within our application. Our search service will be robust, user-friendly, and production-ready by the end.

CHAPTER 9

Incorporating Vector Search Functionality

You've made significant progress. At this point in your learning journey, you've built a fully functioning vector search utility in a robust Node.js back end, explored the theory behind vector search, and learned the math and algorithms that power it. Take pride in how far you've come.

In the remaining chapters, we'll focus on integrating and optimizing your vector search functionality for real-world use. This chapter begins that process by adding a search API to your back end. We'll cover rate limiting, error handling, and structuring requests and responses to ensure a smooth and efficient search experience. By the end, you'll have a fully functioning search API built on the vector search service you've created.

Understanding the Current API Service Layer

Our application's API service layer serves as the bridge between the client-side interface and the back-end functionality. It's designed to manage user requests, enforce security, and handle data transactions efficiently. As we prepare to incorporate a vector search API into this architecture, you must understand how the current API structure works.

Each route file uses Express Router instances to define and group endpoints. For example, in articleRoutes.js, we see routes for endpoints such as /feed and /:slug. Each route associates an endpoint with a specific controller function from the articlesController.js file, which encapsulates the business logic needed for each operation.

Security is a crucial aspect of the API service layer, especially in applications that involve user authentication and authorization. For this purpose, the application uses middleware functions like verifyJWT to enforce access control on specific routes. The verifyJWT middleware, located in the middleware/ folder, checks for a valid JSON Web Token (JWT) in the authorization header of each incoming request. The user's identity is verified if the token is valid, and their details are made accessible in subsequent controller functions.

This modular structure will serve us well as we move forward in this chapter to design and implement a search API for our vector search functionality. We'll create a dedicated route file for the search functionality and define endpoints that enable users to perform vector-based searches. We can integrate this new feature without disrupting the existing architecture by maintaining a clear separation between routes, controllers, and middleware.

If that's a lot of text, then it's a good time for a visualization to help you understand the structure of the API service layer. Please take a look at the following diagram to see how the routes, controllers, and middleware interact within the API service layer of our application.

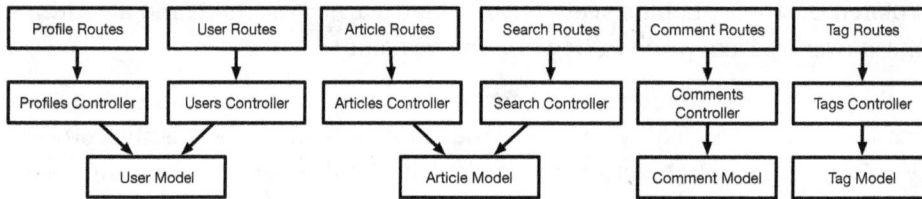

With this foundation in place, we're ready to explore the specifics of designing our new search functionality. In the following pages, we'll explore how to add a dedicated vector search API endpoint, integrate it seamlessly into this architecture, and leverage our vector search index to provide fast, relevant search results. Let's get started with designing the new search endpoint.

Designing the Search API Endpoint

The API endpoint will serve as the gateway through which users submit search queries and receive contextually relevant results based on the vector search index we previously set up in Couchbase. Designing this endpoint is more than simply returning results; it's about building a user-friendly, efficient, and resilient search experience that meets performance and security expectations.

We'll use the POST method for our search endpoint, allowing us to pass search parameters such as the query string, limit, and offset in the request body. Passing parameters in the body provides flexibility for handling longer queries and filters that would be cumbersome in a URL.

Although POST is typically not idempotent in REST APIs, our search endpoint should still behave in an idempotent way. A request qualifies as *idempotent* if sending it multiple times produces the same outcome as sending it once. In the search case, repeated identical requests should return the same results without side effects or changes to the server state.

To support idempotency, we'll design our search API to be stateless. Each request will operate independently, using only the parameters provided, and will not depend on any previous requests. A stateless approach ensures that retries or repeated calls always return consistent, predictable results.

Next, let's examine the structure of the request payload and the parameters we expect to receive.

The main parameter for our search endpoint is query, the user's search string. The system converts this string into a vector embedding and compares it to stored embeddings. Optional parameters such as limit and offset support pagination and control result size, making the endpoint flexible for both quick lookups and deeper browsing.

The response will be a structured JSON object containing an array of articles ranked by similarity. Each result will include metadata such as title, summary, and similarity score to help the front end present beneficial, relevant results.

Users aren't perfect, and neither are the systems we build for them. Our API must handle errors gracefully, whether due to accidental input or malicious behavior. It will return meaningful error messages and appropriate status codes to provide clear feedback. For example, the system returns a 400 Bad Request if the query parameter is missing or malformed. If a server-side error occurs, the API will respond with a 500 Internal Server Error and log the details on the back end for further analysis.

As we've discussed, generating embeddings and calculating similarity scores is resource intensive. To prevent abuse and protect performance, we'll implement rate limiting on the search API. This restricts how many requests a user can make within a given time frame, ensuring fair usage. By enforcing reasonable limits, we keep the API responsive, reduce back-end strain, and manage resource consumption more effectively.

Let's see a visual flow of how our new vector search API endpoint will be structured. The diagram on page 90 provides a high-level overview of the request and response flow, illustrating the key components and interactions in processing a search query.

This diagram captures the request-response cycle for the search API. The client sends a search query in a POST request, which first passes through input validation. Once validated, the search query is processed, transformed

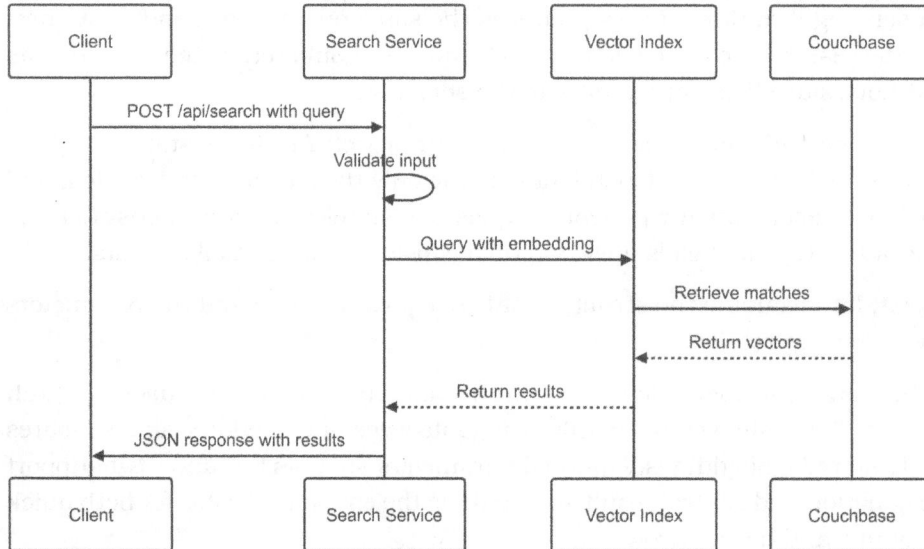

into a vector embedding, and sent to our vector index. The database service performs the similarity calculations and returns the matching results, which the API then structures into a user-friendly JSON format before sending it back to the client.

With a clear understanding of the endpoint's purpose and flow, we're prepared to move forward into the actual implementation phase. This work will bring our theoretical design to life, enabling real-time, efficient vector search for our application's users.

Implementing the Search API Endpoint

It's time to translate our design into a functional endpoint, following the structure of the existing application and adhering to best practices for code organization, readability, and maintainability.

Preparing the Search Route

The first step in implementing the search API is to add a new route in the routes/ directory. This route will direct incoming POST requests for search queries to the appropriate controller method. To ensure consistency with the rest of the application, we'll create a new file, searchRoutes.js, in the routes/ directory. Here's what the initial route file might look like:

incorporating_vector_search_functionality/searchRoutes.js
```
import express from 'express';
import { performSearch } from '../controllers/searchController';
```

```
const router = express.Router();

// Route for performing vector search
router.post('/', performSearch);

export default router;
```

This setup ensures all incoming search requests are routed directly to the performSearch controller method, streamlining access to the search functionality.

Creating the Search Controller

Next, we implement the search API's core logic in a new searchController.js file within the controllers/ directory. This file will define the performSearch function, which handles incoming requests, validates inputs, and interfaces with the database to fetch results from the vector search index.

Here's an initial implementation of the controller:

```
incorporating_vector_search_functionality/searchController.js
import asyncHandler from 'express-async-handler';
import { Query, getDefaultInstance } from 'ottoman';
import { Logger } from '../config/logger';

const log = Logger.child({ namespace: 'searchController' });

const performSearch = asyncHandler(async (req, res) => {
  const { query } = req.body;

  // Validate the presence of query input
  if (!query || typeof query !== 'string') {
    log.debug('Invalid or missing search query');
    return res.status(400).json({
      message: 'Search query is required and must be a string',
    });
  }

  log.debug(`Received search query: ${query}`);

  try {
    // Build the vector search query for Couchbase
    const couchbaseQuery = new Query(
      {
        where: {
          embedding: {
            $similarity: {
              query: query,
              metric: 'dot_product',
            },
          },
        },
        limit: 10,
      },
```

```
    'articles'
  ).build();

  log.debug(`Generated Couchbase query: ${couchbaseQuery}`);

  // Execute the query using Ottoman.js
  const ottoman = getDefaultInstance();
  const { rows } = await ottoman.query(couchbaseQuery);

  // Structure and return results
  const results = rows.map(row => ({
    id: row.id,
    title: row.title,
    description: row.description,
  }));

    return res.status(200).json({ results, count: results.length });
  } catch (error) {
    log.error(error, 'Error performing vector search');
    return res.status(500).json({
      message: 'An error occurred while processing the search',
    });
  }
});

export { performSearch };
```

This implementation ensures that the search functionality is accessible to all users while addressing three critical aspects of back-end service development: *input validation*, *structured logging*, and *error handling*. Let's look at how the performSearch controller manages each one.

Before performing any database operations, the controller checks the validity of the incoming search query. Specifically, it ensures that the query field is a string present in the request body.

If the validation fails, the API responds with a 400 Bad Request status code, ensuring users receive clear feedback on what went wrong.

Logging is an indispensable part of any back-end application. In this controller, structured logs capture key events, such as the receipt of a query and the generated database query. Capturing these events helps developers monitor API usage and debug issues effectively. For example, this snippet from the controller logs the search query received from the user:

```
log.debug(`Received search query: ${query}`);
```

Finally, the controller includes error handling to manage unexpected issues during the search process. If an error occurs while querying the database or processing results, the API responds with a 500 Internal Server Error status code, indicating a server-side problem. The system logs the error details for further investigation, helping developers quickly identify and resolve issues.

Bringing It All Together

With the route and controller in place, the final step is integrating the new route into the application. Update the api/index.js file to include searchRoutes:

```
incorporating_vector_search_functionality/api/index.js
import searchRoutes from '../routes/searchRoutes';
app.use('/api/search', searchRoutes);
```

This integration makes the new search endpoint part of the application's API, allowing users to submit search queries and receive results seamlessly.

Let's examine a visual representation of the search API endpoint flow. The following diagram illustrates the request-response cycle for the search functionality, highlighting the key components and interactions involved in processing a search query.

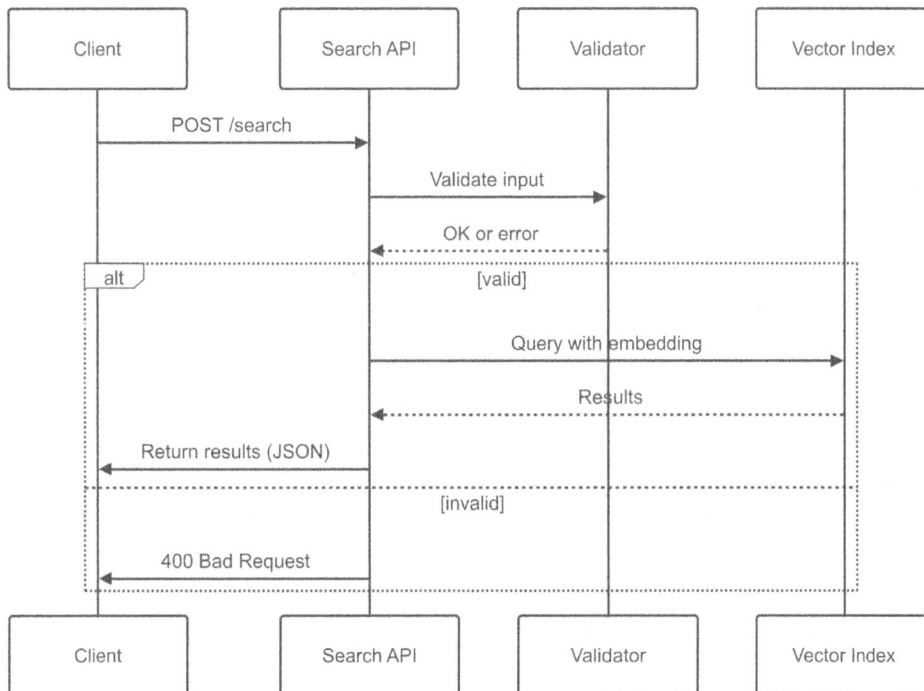

With the search API endpoint implemented, we've successfully integrated vector search functionality into our application's back end. Users can submit search queries, and the API will return relevant articles based on the vector similarity calculations performed in Couchbase. This step marks a significant milestone in our journey to build a robust, production-ready search service that leverages the power of vector search.

In the next section, we'll explore how to handle errors and validations in the search API, ensuring that users receive clear feedback and that the service remains reliable and secure.

Managing Rate Limiting and Security Considerations

As we expand the capabilities of the search API, ensuring its stability and security becomes paramount. Managing rate limiting and addressing security concerns are crucial to maintaining the service's integrity, reliability, and usability, especially as it scales to accommodate larger user bases.

Rate limiting is a technique for controlling the number of requests a client can make to the API within a specified time frame. Without it, a single client or a group of clients could inadvertently or maliciously overwhelm the server, leading to degraded performance or even downtime. By imposing limits, we ensure fair resource distribution among users and safeguard the back end from abuse.

In our search API, middleware monitors incoming requests and enforces rate limiting based on criteria such as client IP addresses or API keys. When a client exceeds the defined limits, the middleware can respond with an error message, such as "Too many search requests from this IP, please try again after a minute," and log the incident for further analysis. This approach helps maintain service availability, protect against abuse, and provide valuable insights into usage patterns.

Here's an example of rate-limiting middleware:

```
incorporating_vector_search_functionality/rateLimiter.js
import rateLimit from 'express-rate-limit';

const searchRateLimiter = rateLimit({
  windowMs: 60 * 1000, // 1-minute window
  max: 30, // Limit each IP to 30 requests per windowMs
  message: 'Too many search requests, please try again in a minute.',
  handler: (req, res, next, options) => {
    log.warn(`Rate limit exceeded for IP: ${req.ip}`);
    res.status(429).json({ error: options.message });
  }
});

export default searchRateLimiter;
```

This middleware, built with the express-rate-limit npm package, restricts clients to a reasonable number of search requests per minute. It also logs incidents of rate-limit breaches, providing valuable data for monitoring and auditing. Applying this middleware to the search API route is as simple as wrapping it around the route definition:

```
router.get('/search', searchRateLimiter, searchController.searchArticles);
```

Rate limiting is just one piece of the puzzle. Security considerations for a public-facing API extend beyond managing request frequency. We must address several key areas to protect the search API, including injection attacks and resilience against distributed denial-of-service (DDoS) attacks.

Search APIs are particularly vulnerable to injection attacks, where bad actors craft malicious input to manipulate back-end operations. Although our API uses Ottoman.js to query the Couchbase database, it's crucial to rigorously validate and sanitize all inputs. The validateText function that we built earlier in the services/utils folder, for example, ensures that query strings, limits, and offsets conform to expected formats and prevent harmful payloads.

Having these validation functions in place ensures that user inputs are sanitized and validated before being processed and sent to the database. This helps prevent malicious activities that could compromise the integrity of the search service. Using parameterized queries in Ottoman.js adds an extra layer of protection by separating input values from query logic, thus neutralizing attempts to inject rogue commands into the database.

In addition to injection attacks, DDoS attacks pose a significant threat to API availability. These attacks flood the server with high requests, overwhelming its capacity and causing downtime. To mitigate this risk, we can employ DDoS protection services, such as Cloudflare or AWS Shield, which filter incoming traffic and block malicious requests before they reach the server. These services use sophisticated algorithms to detect and respond to DDoS attacks in real time, ensuring that the search API remains accessible and responsive to legitimate users.

Many resources are out there to help you understand and implement these security measures. To learn more about security best practices, you can check out the OWASP API Security Top 10,[1] which provides a comprehensive guide to securing APIs against common threats.

By implementing rate limiting and addressing security concerns, we fortify the search API against misuse and malicious activities, ensuring it remains stable, performant, and secure. When combined with robust error handling

---

1. https://owasp.org/www-project-api-security/

and structured logging, these measures create a resilient back-end service that can handle a wide range of search requests while protecting user data and maintaining service availability.

Key Takeaways

In this chapter, we took significant steps to bring vector search functionality to life in our application. By building a dedicated search API, we've bridged the gap between the back end and the user experience, enabling fast and relevant search results powered by the vector search index created earlier. We explored critical concepts along the way, from designing RESTful endpoints to implementing robust input validation, rate limiting, and security measures.

These are the key takeaways:

- *Understanding the API service layer*: We revisited the structure of our application's API layer, emphasizing the roles of routes, controllers, and middleware, which laid the foundation for integrating the new search endpoint.

- *Designing and implementing the search API*: We applied RESTful principles to create an intuitive, idempotent search endpoint, ensuring flexibility for future enhancements and consistency with the existing architecture.

- *Error handling and security*: We emphasized the importance of structured error handling, robust input validation, and defensive programming practices to safeguard the API against misuse and ensure a seamless user experience.

- *Rate limiting and stability*: By incorporating rate-limiting mechanisms, we protected the service against overuse while maintaining fair user access.

In the next chapter, we'll focus on further enhancing the search functionality, diving into optimization techniques that refine accuracy, handle complex queries, and prepare the service for real-world demands.

CHAPTER 10

Optimizing Search Results

You've covered much on your journey into vector search—from theory and algorithms to building a working search service. Now you're ready to take your search experience even further. In this chapter, you'll enhance your search by integrating weighted rankings to incorporate factors like popularity and recency, optimizing query efficiency by handling *stop words*, and introducing hybrid search to leverage vector and keyword-based approaches.

Search is not only about matching queries to results but also about ensuring those results align closely with user intent and expectations. Adding weighted ranking will deliver more relevant and timely results, while tackling stop words will improve search precision. Additionally, a hybrid search system will ensure your application intelligently chooses between vector and keyword searches, offering users the most effective results. Let's get started by exploring weighted ranking.

Weighted Ranking

As users interact with search applications, their expectations go beyond simple matches. They seek results that feel timely, impactful, and aligned with their intent. While vector similarity is a powerful mechanism for matching concepts, it's often insufficient to provide a complete picture of relevance. We can combine vector similarity with external factors like recency and popularity by incorporating weighted rankings to create a richer, more intuitive search experience.

Consider the query "latest advancements in AI." A stand-alone vector search might prioritize articles based solely on their conceptual similarity to the query. However, if some of these articles are outdated or have had little engagement, they may not be the most useful to the user. Weighted ranking helps address this by introducing additional criteria influencing how results are sorted and presented. In this chapter, we'll focus on two such criteria:

- *Recency*: Prioritizing articles published more recently to ensure that users see the latest content.

- *Popularity*: Factoring in metrics such as views, likes, or shares to highlight articles that have garnered significant user interest.

Together, these signals augment the vector similarity score, creating a balanced ranking system that accounts for conceptual relevance and user-driven context.

Calculating and Storing Ranking Metrics

Before integrating recency and popularity into our search ranking, we must calculate and store these metrics for each article in our database. Let's start with recency. You can derive this metric from the publication date of an article. We'll represent recency as the number of days since the article was published, inversely scaled so that newer articles have higher scores, like this for example:

```
recency = max_days - (current_date - publication_date)
```

Here, max_days is a constant representing the maximum time period considered relevant (such as 365 days for one year). Articles older than this range will have a recency score of zero. To calculate this value, we'll update the logic in our data model as follows:

```
optimizing_search_results/updated_article_model.js
ArticleSchema.pre('save', function (next) {
  const currentDate = new Date();
  const maxDays = 365;
  const publicationDate = this.publicationDate || currentDate;

  this.recency = Math.max(
    0,
    maxDays - Math.floor(
      (currentDate - publicationDate) / (1000 * 60 * 60 * 24)
    )
  );

  next();
});
```

Next, let's address popularity. This metric can be computed based on engagement data, such as the number of views or likes an article has received. For simplicity, we'll define popularity as a weighted sum of these factors:

```
popularity = (0.7 * views) + (0.3 * likes)
```

Similar to recency, we'll calculate and store this value in the article document. Whenever an article is viewed or liked, we'll update its popularity score using an event-driven approach or a periodic batch-update process, depending on the application's needs. We'll leave it to you to implement this aspect of user engagement tracking in your application.

Once these fields are integrated into the database, our articles will have three key metrics: similarity_score, recency, and popularity, which can be used to rank search results. With these fields, we have the foundation for incorporating weighted ranking into our search API.

Integrating Weighted Ranking in the Search API

With the necessary fields in place, we can modify the search API to incorporate weighted ranking. Let's revisit our ranking formula:

```
final_score = (0.7 * similarity_score) + (0.2 * recency) + (0.1 * popularity)
```

Let's explain this formula in plain English. The final_score is a weighted sum of three components: similarity_score, recency, and popularity. The similarity_score is the primary factor, accounting for 70 percent of the final score. Recency and popularity contribute 20 percent and 10 percent, respectively. This distribution ensures that vector similarity remains the primary ranking factor, while recency and popularity provide additional context.

Adjust these weights based on your application's specific requirements. For example, if recency is more critical than popularity, you could increase its weight in the formula. The key is to experiment with different weightings to find the balance that best suits your users' needs.

To implement this, we'll update our controller's performSearch method.

```
optimizing_search_results/updated_performSearch.js
import asyncHandler from 'express-async-handler';
import { Query, getDefaultInstance } from 'ottoman';

const performSearch = asyncHandler(async (req, res) => {
  const { query } = req.body;

  if (!query || typeof query !== 'string') {
    return res.status(400).json({
      message: 'Search query is required and must be a string',
    });
  }

  const searchQuery = new Query(
    {
      where: {
        embedding: {
```

```
          $similarity: {
            query: query,
            metric: 'dot_product',
          },
        },
      },
      orderBy: [{ final_score: 'DESC' }],
      limit: 10,
    },
    'articles'
).build();

const ottoman = getDefaultInstance();
const { rows } = await ottoman.query(searchQuery);

return res.status(200).json({
  results: rows.map((row) => ({
    id: row.id,
    title: row.title,
    description: row.description,
    final_score: row.final_score,
  })),
  count: rows.length,
});
});

export { performSearch };
```

Here, the final_score field is calculated on the database side using the stored values for similarity, recency, and popularity. This approach offloads the ranking logic to the database, reducing back-end complexity and improving performance.

From the user's perspective, weighted ranking ensures they immediately see results that are semantically relevant but also timely and popular. For example, if your site offers technical tutorials, users will first see recent, trending articles with current implementation advice. Without weighted ranking, users might need to search through older results to find the most current information.

Understanding Stop Words

While weighted ranking improves result prioritization, the quality of the query still determines how effective those results are. Stop words, such as *the*, *is*, and *and*, can introduce noise into vector embeddings, reducing the precision of search results. For example, the query "the rise of AI" might be less effective than "rise AI" because *the* and *of* contribute little semantic meaning.

However, removing stop words must be done carefully so we don't remove important context from a query. For instance, the word *to* might be a stop word in general text but critical in a query like "how to code."

Effective stop-word removal requires more than a static list; it must consider the context. For instance, common phrases like "how to" carry essential meaning, especially in technical tutorials, and should be preserved during preprocessing to maintain query accuracy.

The real-world impact of context-aware stop-word removal is clear. A large IT consultancy team building an internal vector search system for closed support tickets found their search failed whenever queries involved negation. Their system removed crucial words without considering context, leading to irrelevant results. Addressing this required analyzing how stop words appeared in actual queries and adjusting their approach accordingly, greatly improving accuracy.

In our implementation, we preprocess queries by first detecting predefined meaningful phrases. If such phrases appear, we preserve them entirely; otherwise, we remove stop words selectively, respecting exceptions critical to our application. This preprocessing occurs before generating vector embeddings, resulting in more precise and relevant search results.

Let's implement and integrate this improved stop-word handling into our vector search API.

Implementing Stop-Word Removal

Place the stop-word removal logic in a new file named stopWordProcessor.js inside the utils/ directory within the services/ folder. This file exports a single function, processQuery, which accepts a raw user query and returns a cleaned query string.

You'll find many different ways to implement this logic, but the following simple example will get you started.

```
optimizing_search_results/stopWordProcessor.js
const preservedPhrases = [
  "how to",
  "learn to",
  "step by step",
];
```

```javascript
const stopWords = new Set([
  "a",
  "an",
  "the",
  "is",
  "of",
  "on",
  "to",
  "in",
  "for",
  "by",
  "with",
  "and",
  "or",
]);

/**
 * Processes a query string by removing stop words and preserving key phrases.
 * @param {string} query - The raw query string from the user.
 * @returns {string} - The processed query string.
 */
const processQuery = (query) => {
  if (typeof query !== "string") {
    throw new Error("Query must be a string");
  }

  // Normalize the query to lowercase for consistent processing
  const normalizedQuery = query.toLowerCase();

  // Check for preserved phrases
  for (const phrase of preservedPhrases) {
    if (normalizedQuery.includes(phrase)) {
      // Return the original query if a preserved phrase is found
      return query;
    }
  }

  // Tokenize the query into words
  const words = query.split(/\s+/);

  // Filter out stop words, preserving all non-stop words
  const filteredWords =
    words.filter((word) => !stopWords.has(word.toLowerCase()));

  // Reconstruct the query string
  const cleanedQuery = filteredWords.join(" ");

  return cleanedQuery;
};

export { processQuery };
```

Let's break this code example down in plain English. The processQuery function takes a raw user query as input and returns a cleaned query string. It first normalizes the query to lowercase for consistent processing. It then checks for predefined preserved phrases in the query. If the function finds a preserved phrase, it returns the original query to maintain its integrity. If it doesn't find preserved phrases, it tokenizes the query into individual words and filters out any stop words. The function then reconstructs the remaining words into a cleaned query string and returns it to the caller.

As we mentioned, by doing this preprocessing work at the earliest stage of query handling, we ensure that all the subsequent operations, from embedding generation to database queries, benefit from cleaner and more precise input. Preprocessing at this stage is critical in enhancing the relevance and accuracy of our search results. As an additional significant benefit, reducing the size of the query embedding can also reduce computational overhead, which, depending on how you've architected your system, can save on machine resources and cost.

Incorporating Stop-Word Removal in the Search Pipeline

Once you implement the utility, incorporate it into the search API pipeline. Run the preprocessing step before transforming the query string into a vector embedding to ensure the system uses the cleaned query in subsequent operations.

To achieve this, modify the performSearch function in the searchController.js file to use the processQuery utility. Here's the updated code:

```
optimizing_search_results/performSearch_with_search_method_routing.js
import asyncHandler from 'express-async-handler';
import { Query } from 'ottoman';
import { Logger } from '../config/logger';
import { processQuery } from '../services/utils/stopWordProcessor';

const log = Logger.child({ namespace: 'searchController' });

const performSearch = asyncHandler(async (req, res) => {
  const { query } = req.body;

  // Validate the presence of the query input
  if (!query || typeof query !== 'string') {
    log.debug('Invalid or missing search query');
    return res.status(400).json({
      message: 'Search query is required and must be a string',
    });
  }
```

```
log.debug(`Received raw search query: ${query}`);

// Preprocess the query to remove stop words
const cleanedQuery = processQuery(query);

log.debug(`Cleaned search query: ${cleanedQuery}`);

// Determine the search method based on query type
const searchMethod = cleanedQuery.includes('"') ? 'exact' : 'conceptual';

log.debug(`Detected search method: ${searchMethod}`);

try {
  // Route the query to the appropriate search module
  if (searchMethod === 'exact') {
    // Perform keyword-based search
    // Implement keyword search logic here
  } else {
    // Perform vector-based search
    // Implement vector search logic here
  }

  // Return search results
  return res.status(200).json({ results: [], count: 0 });
} catch (error) {
  log.error(error, 'Error performing search');
  return res.status(500).json({
    message: 'An error occurred while processing the search',
  });
}
});
export { performSearch };
```

First, we import the processQuery utility from the stopWordProcessor.js file. We then call this utility to clean the raw query string before proceeding with the search operation. The system uses the cleaned query to generate the vector search query, removing stop words and focusing on relevant terms.

By integrating stop-word removal into our search pipeline, we've sharpened the focus of user queries, delivering more relevant results without losing essential context. This improvement optimizes our vector search service and lays a solid foundation for future enhancements.

Optimizing Results with a Hybrid Search System

Hybrid search is another effective optimization technique that complements vector search by combining its semantic strengths with traditional keyword matching. Vector embeddings excel at understanding concepts but may not always be ideal for specific searches, such as locating an exact article title or author. In these cases, integrating keyword searches can significantly improve precision and user satisfaction by quickly pinpointing exact matches.

To build a hybrid search system, we'll create a mechanism that dynamically selects between vector and keyword methods based on the query type. You can implement this flexibility through user-driven options, such as letting users search explicitly "by author" or "by topic," or through automated logic that detects query intent. Offering both approaches ensures relevant results, streamlines the search experience, and optimizes the platform's performance.

Defining Search Method Selection Criteria

The first step in building a hybrid search system is to define the criteria for when to use vector search versus keyword search. Base these criteria on the characteristics of the query and the desired search experience. For example, you might consider the following factors:

- *Query length*: Short queries with specific terms indicate a keyword search is more appropriate, while longer queries with broader concepts could benefit from vector search.

- *Query structure*: The system might trigger keyword searches for queries containing specific keywords or phrases, while it could route general terms to vector search.

- *User preferences*: The system could allow users to choose their search method and select the approach that best fits their needs.

You establish a foundation for building a flexible and user-centric hybrid search system by defining clear criteria for selecting the search method. These criteria will guide the logic that evaluates user queries and determines the appropriate search module.

One important consideration is to resist the urge to overengineer a solution. While building a complex system that dynamically switches between search methods based on many factors may be tempting, simplicity is often the best approach. By focusing on a few key criteria, or even a single criterion, that align with user needs and application goals, you can create a hybrid search system that is both effective and maintainable.

To avoid overengineering, we can start with a simple distinction: users either perform an *exact* search—they look for a specific article or author—or do a *conceptual* search based on a topic or idea. While other applications may require more complex criteria like query length or structure, this binary approach works well for a blog platform and offers a practical starting point.

Routing Queries to the Appropriate Search Module

With the search method selection criteria defined, we can now implement the logic for routing queries to the appropriate search module. We'll distinguish between exact and conceptual searches to determine whether to use vector or keyword searches.

To achieve this, we'll update the performSearch function in the searchController.js file to evaluate the query and route it to the correct search module. Here's the updated part of the file with pseudo-code describing where to implement the logic for a hybrid switch:

```
optimizing_search_results/performSearch_with_search_method_routing.js
// Determine the search method based on query type
const searchMethod = cleanedQuery.includes('"') ? 'exact' : 'conceptual';

log.debug(`Detected search method: ${searchMethod}`);

try {
  // Route the query to the appropriate search module
  if (searchMethod === 'exact') {
    // Perform keyword-based search
    // Implement keyword search logic here
  } else {
    // Perform vector-based search
    // Implement vector search logic here
  }

  // Return search results
  return res.status(200).json({ results: [], count: 0 });
```

In this updated code snippet, we first preprocess the query by using the processQuery utility to remove stop words. We then evaluate the cleaned query to determine the search method based on whether it contains quotation marks (indicating an exact search) or not (indicating a conceptual search). The system stores the search method in the searchMethod variable and routes the query to the appropriate search module.

We know how to complete the vector-based search as part of the else block, but how do we implement the keyword-based search? We'll leave that as an exercise for you to complete. You can use traditional search techniques like full-text search to implement the keyword-based search logic. Combining both search methods allows you to create a hybrid search system that provides users with a comprehensive search experience tailored to their needs.

Key Takeaways

In this chapter, we explored optimization techniques, including weighted ranking, intelligent stop-word removal, and hybrid search, to enhance the relevance and performance of our search service. We've built a system that better aligns with user intent by combining vector similarity with external signals, refining query precision, and flexibly routing between keyword and vector methods.

Here are the key takeaways:

- Dynamic metrics like recency and popularity can be calculated and stored in the database to create a more nuanced ranking system, ensuring users see timely and relevant results.

- Preprocessing user queries with stop-word removal enhances the quality of vector embeddings and reduces computational overhead.

- Exception handling and preserved phrases during stop-word removal ensure that critical context is not lost, maintaining the intent of the user's query.

- Hybrid search systems allow seamless integration of both vector-based and keyword-based methods, offering flexibility for diverse user requirements.

- A modular utility for stop-word removal ensures reusable, maintainable code that adapts to evolving application needs.

- Routing queries dynamically based on predefined criteria simplifies the hybrid search implementation while keeping the user experience intuitive and efficient.

You've now built a refined and efficient vector search system focused on accuracy, relevance, and user experience. Next, we'll wrap up our time together by exploring practical applications built with vector search today.

CHAPTER 11

Practical Applications and Next Steps

In this book we've explored the fundamentals of vector search and learned how to build a vector search system from scratch. We've covered many topics, from understanding vector embeddings and setting up the environment to implementing vector generation services and creating vector search indexes. We've also discussed incorporating vector search functionality into applications, optimizing search results, and testing and monitoring the system for performance and reliability.

As we conclude this journey, it's essential to reflect on the key takeaways and consider the future of vector search technology. The search field is rapidly evolving, driven by advancements in machine learning, artificial intelligence, and natural language processing. Researchers and engineers constantly develop new techniques and algorithms to improve search accuracy, relevance, and efficiency.

First, before we explore what's next, take a moment to celebrate how far you've come. This technology includes jargon that often intimidates newcomers and even seasoned developers. But you've made it through the book and built a vector search system from scratch. That's no small feat! As a reminder, the source code for the application is available on GitHub,[1] so you can always refer back to it as you continue to explore and learn more about vector search. In addition to the GitHub repository, make sure to bookmark the web page for the book,[2] as it will be updated with new resources and information to keep you informed about the latest developments in vector search technology.

The world of vector search continues to evolve, driven by advancements in machine learning, artificial intelligence, and computational efficiency. As we

---

1. https://github.com/hummusonrails/vector-example-blog-platform
2. https://pragprog.com/titles/bgvector

conclude this book, let's turn our attention to the future of vector search and its exciting possibilities.

Exploring Upcoming New Developments

The field of vector search is rapidly evolving, with new techniques, algorithms, and tools emerging regularly. As you continue your journey, staying informed about these advancements will help ensure your systems remain efficient, relevant, and competitive.

The Promise of Federated Learning

Federated learning trains models across multiple devices or institutions without centralizing the data. Instead of sending raw data to a central server, it shares only model updates, preserving user privacy.

This opens the door for privacy-preserving personalization in vector search. A phone could, for instance, train a model locally on a user's preferences without transmitting private data. This model can then inform more relevant and secure search results.

To learn more, check out TensorFlow Federated,[3] Google's illustrated overview,[4] and recent research exploring federated learning for advanced query processing.[5]

Advancements in Vector Quantization

Vector quantization reduces the size of vector representations, enabling faster similarity calculations. Recent innovations in locally adaptive vector quantization (LVQ) optimize this process by dynamically adjusting granularity based on data density.

This technique is especially valuable for real-time applications like fraud detection and recommendation engines. For a deeper dive, see Qdrant's intro,[6] a PyTorch library for experimentation,[7] Intel's scalable implementation,[8] and a hands-on tutorial from GeeksForGeeks.[9]

---

3. https://www.tensorflow.org/federated
4. https://federated.withgoogle.com/
5. https://arxiv.org/html/2408.05242v1
6. https://qdrant.tech/articles/what-is-vector-quantization
7. https://github.com/lucidrains/vector-quantize-pytorch
8. https://github.com/intel/ScalableVectorSearch
9. https://www.geeksforgeeks.org/learning-vector-quantization/

Searching Offline First

Offline-first search prioritizes functionality even in low- or no-connectivity environments. By storing indexes locally and syncing with the server when possible, applications can remain usable and responsive regardless of network conditions.

Learn more from the Offline-First GitHub project,[10] a tutorial on vector search on iOS,[11] and an article on edge-based search with Couchbase Mobile.[12]

Taking a Look at Real-World Use Cases

Vector search transforms industries by enabling smarter, faster, and more relevant search experiences. Its flexibility allows teams to apply it across various fields, from financial services to entertainment. In this section, we'll explore three distinct use cases that illustrate the power of vector search in real-world scenarios. Each example highlights how vector search solves critical business challenges, drives innovation, and creates value for organizations.

Fraud Detection in Financial Services

Fraud prevention is a top priority for financial institutions, where the stakes are high and the window to detect and respond to threats is narrow. Revolut, a leading Fintech company, uses vector search to power its fraud detection system, Sherlock.[13]

Sherlock analyzes real-time transaction patterns and identifies anomalies that could indicate fraudulent behavior. The system converts each transaction into a vector, capturing features like amount, merchant, location, and time. It compares these vectors to historical patterns and flags transactions as fraudulent if a match suggests suspicious behavior, often within 50 milliseconds.

Vector search, machine learning, and an optimized database architecture deliver this speed. Couchbase stores user and merchant profiles, enabling fast retrieval and real-time responses. The team continually updates Sherlock with new models to stay ahead of emerging threats.

---

10. https://github.com/pazguille/offline-first
11. https://alessandrocauduro.medium.com/building-ai-powered-vector-search-on-iphone-996b1502f4aa
12. https://www.couchbase.com/blog/vector-search-at-the-edge-with-couchbase-mobile/
13. https://medium.com/revolut/building-a-state-of-the-art-card-fraud-detection-system-in-9-months-96463d7f652d

Personalized Music Content Recommendations

Spotify, a global leader in music streaming, uses vector search to power its recommendation engine.[14] Personalized playlists like Discover Weekly and Release Radar rely on vector embeddings that represent both users and content.

User vectors are built from listening habits, liked songs, and playlist interactions. Content vectors represent musical traits like genre, tempo, and artist similarity. Spotify compares these vectors in real time to surface highly relevant music and podcast recommendations.

This dynamic recommendation system keeps users engaged while showcasing vector search's performance and personalization benefits.

Enhanced Customer Support

Zendesk, a major player in the customer-support software space, leverages vector search to improve its knowledge base and ticket-resolution systems.[15]

When a customer submits a support ticket or searches the help center, their query is converted into a vector and matched against support content. This semantic similarity approach returns relevant results even when the query uses a language different from the stored content.

For example, a question like "How do I reset my password?" might return documents titled "Password Recovery Steps" or "Account Login Help." Delivering semantically relevant results in this way leads to faster resolution times, improved customer satisfaction, and reduced agent workload.

You have made it to the end of this journey, and that is no small achievement. You've navigated complex ideas, implemented practical code, and built a fully functioning vector search system from scratch. Whether you're a seasoned developer or new to this domain, you now have the tools, understanding, and confidence to integrate vector search into real-world projects. Please take a moment to appreciate how far you've come; you've earned it.

Whether holding a physical copy of this book or reading a digital edition, the content here represents a final, committed version. However, your journey with vector search doesn't end here! The resources shared on the book's

---

14. https://engineering.atspotify.com/2023/10/introducing-voyager-spotifys-new-nearest-neighbor-search-library/
15. https://www.zendesk.com/blog/ai-customer-service/

website at vectorsearchbook.com[16] and the web page for this book on Prag-Prog[17] are being updated regularly as the technology continues to progress. I encourage you to stay connected, explore the latest developments, and use the growing collection of tools and insights. Thank you for joining me on this adventure. I'm excited to see where your exploration of vector search takes you next!

---

16. https://www.vectorsearchbook.com
17. https://pragprog.com/titles/bgvector

Thank you!

We hope you enjoyed this book and that you're already thinking about what you want to learn next. To help make that decision easier, we're offering you this gift.

Head on over to https://pragprog.com right now, and use the coupon code BUYANOTHER2025 to save 30% on your next ebook. Offer is void where prohibited or restricted. This offer does not apply to any edition of *The Pragmatic Programmer* ebook.

And if you'd like to share your own expertise with the world, why not propose a writing idea to us? After all, many of our best authors started off as our readers, just like you. With up to a 50% royalty, world-class editorial services, and a name you trust, there's nothing to lose. Visit https://pragprog.com/become-an-author/ today to learn more and to get started.

Thank you for your continued support. We hope to hear from you again soon!

The Pragmatic Bookshelf

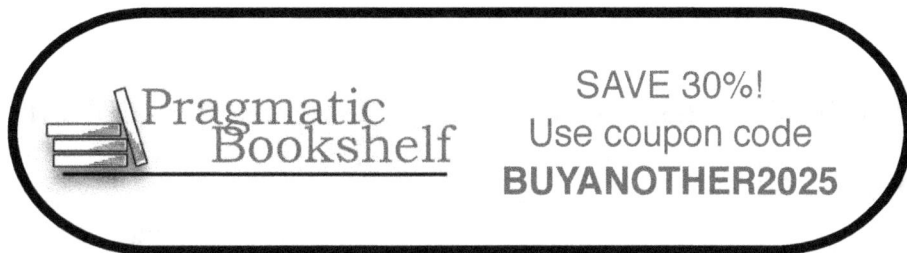

Pragmatic Bookshelf

SAVE 30%!
Use coupon code
BUYANOTHER2025

A Common-Sense Guide to Data Structures and Algorithms in JavaScript, Volume 1

If you thought data structures and algorithms were all just theory, you're missing out on what they can do for your JavaScript code. Learn to use Big O notation to make your code run faster by orders of magnitude. Choose from data structures such as hash tables, trees, and graphs to increase your code's efficiency exponentially. With simple language and clear diagrams, this book makes this complex topic accessible, no matter your background. Every chapter features practice exercises to give you the hands-on information you need to master data structures and algorithms for your day-to-day work.

Jay Wengrow
(514 pages) ISBN: 9798888650646. $69.95
https://pragprog.com/book/jwjavascript

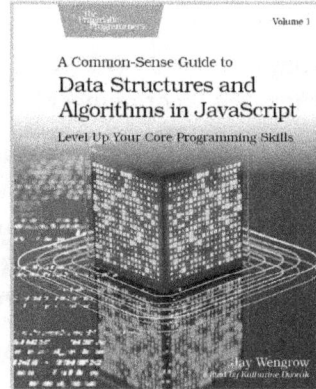

A Common-Sense Guide to Data Structures and Algorithms, Second Edition

If you thought that data structures and algorithms were all just theory, you're missing out on what they can do for your code. Learn to use Big O notation to make your code run faster by orders of magnitude. Choose from data structures such as hash tables, trees, and graphs to increase your code's efficiency exponentially. With simple language and clear diagrams, this book makes this complex topic accessible, no matter your background. This new edition features practice exercises in every chapter, and new chapters on topics such as dynamic programming and heaps and tries. Get the hands-on info you need to master data structures and algorithms for your day-to-day work.

Jay Wengrow
(506 pages) ISBN: 9781680507225. $45.95
https://pragprog.com/book/jwdsal2

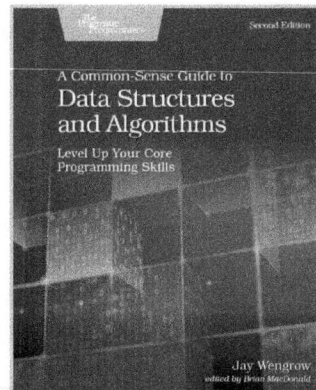

Machine Learning in Elixir

Stable Diffusion, ChatGPT, Whisper—these are just a few examples of incredible applications powered by developments in machine learning. Despite the ubiquity of machine learning applications running in production, there are only a few viable language choices for data science and machine learning tasks. Elixir's Nx project seeks to change that. With Nx, you can leverage the power of machine learning in your applications, using the battle-tested Erlang VM in a pragmatic language like Elixir. In this book, you'll learn how to leverage Elixir and the Nx ecosystem to solve real-world problems in computer vision, natural language processing, and more.

Sean Moriarity
(372 pages) ISBN: 9798888650349. $61.95
https://pragprog.com/book/smelixir

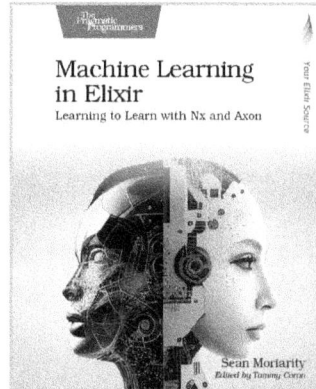

Programming Machine Learning

You've decided to tackle machine learning — because you're job hunting, embarking on a new project, or just think self-driving cars are cool. But where to start? It's easy to be intimidated, even as a software developer. The good news is that it doesn't have to be that hard. Conquer machine learning by writing code one line at a time, from simple learning programs all the way to a true deep learning system. Tackle the hard topics by breaking them down so they're easier to understand, and build your confidence by getting your hands dirty.

Paolo Perrotta
(340 pages) ISBN: 9781680506600. $47.95
https://pragprog.com/book/pplearn

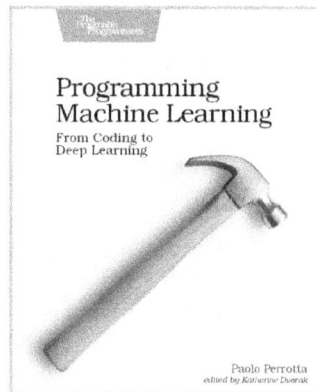

The Pragmatic Bookshelf

The Pragmatic Bookshelf features books written by professional developers for professional developers. The titles continue the well-known Pragmatic Programmer style and continue to garner awards and rave reviews. As development gets more and more difficult, the Pragmatic Programmers will be there with more titles and products to help you stay on top of your game.

Visit Us Online

This Book's Home Page
https://pragprog.com/book/bgvector
Source code from this book, errata, and other resources. Come give us feedback, too!

Keep Up-to-Date
https://pragprog.com
Join our announcement mailing list (low volume) or follow us on Twitter @pragprog for new titles, sales, coupons, hot tips, and more.

New and Noteworthy
https://pragprog.com/news
Check out the latest Pragmatic developments, new titles, and other offerings.

Save on the ebook

Save on the ebook versions of this title. Owning the paper version of this book entitles you to purchase the electronic versions at a terrific discount.

PDFs are great for carrying around on your laptop—they are hyperlinked, have color, and are fully searchable. Most titles are also available for the iPhone and iPod touch, Amazon Kindle, and other popular e-book readers.

Send a copy of your receipt to support@pragprog.com and we'll provide you with a discount coupon.

Contact Us

Online Orders:	*https://pragprog.com/catalog*
Customer Service:	*support@pragprog.com*
International Rights:	*translations@pragprog.com*
Academic Use:	*academic@pragprog.com*
Write for Us:	*http://write-for-us.pragprog.com*